The Autoimmune Personality

Anne Angelone

Anne Angelone

Copyright © by Anne Angelone 2018

ISBN: 9781728826554

All Rights Reserved

Website: www.anneangelone.com

Table of Contents

What are Autoimmune Disorders?

Autoimmune disorders occur when the immune system sets off a reaction to foreign proteins that also inadvertently destroys normal body tissues. While there are well over eighty types of autoimmune diseases, some examples include Multiple Sclerosis, Systemic Lupus Erythematosus, Rheumatoid Arthritis, Ankylosing Spondylitis, Crohn's disease, Type 1 Diabetes and Hashimoto's thyroid disease.

Besides genetic predisposition, we now know that autoimmune diseases are triggered by multiple factors such as stress, infection, emotional reactivity, enhanced cognitive capacity, intestinal permeability, nutrient deficiency, lack of sleep, and food and other environmental sensitivities. All of these factors not only affect immune activity, but also have an effect on emotions and personality. Because of this we need to take everything into account when considering psychological trait manifestations per individual.

Most practitioners in the know are already addressing key issues related to autoimmune flare-ups. So far this has included treating intestinal permeability and shoring up nutrient density for the immune system to function better. It has also included looking at other epigenetic factors such as exercise, sleep and stress reduction. What we have not yet done is explicate the neurobiological underpinnings of personality traits that tend to express in those with autoimmune disease and predispose them to persistent flare-ups.

Personality Traits and Phenotypes

Issues of self, personality, behaviors and dis-ease have been looked at very narrowly until recently. We now know that any input from the environment can impact genetic expression of disease traits as well as personality traits. Personality traits are characteristic patterns of behavior that can either be self-assessed or assessed by others.

Personality traits are multigenic. This means that traits are a combination of inherited genes that are influenced by both nature and nurture. In other words, our personalities have a genetic component, but this doesn't mean that we are born with our personality. Personality is considered a complex trait that is influenced by many different genetic and environmental factors. There is always an interplay of genes and environment – or traits and environment.

Even though some personality traits might be perceived as negative (e.g., distressed) it doesn't mean that this will constantly express (phenotype) unless the exact right stressful conditions line up. The same is true for autoimmune genes, which are also subject to all aspects of our environment that set the stage for those genes to express. One of the biggest challenges for those with autoimmune disease is chronic inflammation impacting gene expression.

Chronic Stress, Inflammation and Personality

All autoimmune diseases share the common thread of chronic inflammation. It is now common knowledge that chronic stress and inflammation generally trigger most diseases to express. We also know that having a disease causes significant stress in many patients, which can lead to other problems. Stress can disrupt both hormonal and neurochemical reactions that impact normal brain function.

Chronic stress and inflammation can also affect personality trait expression, brain atrophy and neurodegeneration. Further, chronic stress and inflammation have been shown to trigger the genetic expression of psychiatric symptoms (e.g., depression, PTSD, anxiety, schizophrenia, aggression associated with antisocial personality disorder, etc.) as well as immune system disorders, including rheumatoid arthritis, systemic lupus erythematosus, multiple sclerosis, Hashimoto's thyroiditis, chronic fatigue syndrome, polymyalgia rheumatica, fibromyalgia and IBS.

Overactive immune responses lead to excessive inflammation, which causes fatigue, joint pain, digestive concerns and lack of mental clarity or brain fog. Any chronic inflammatory or autoimmune disease points toward the fact that the immune system can cause an increase in cytokines that cross the blood brain barrier and inflame the glial cells (which are about 85%) of the brain.

Also, it is now well known that an inflamed and leaky gut leads to an inflamed brain. If your brain is inflamed, it will not be able to signal the vagus nerve, which is housed in the brainstem. Increased neuroinflammation leads to decreased vagal signaling which inevitably leads to high sympathetic tone and fight-flight-freeze responses. When there is untamed inflammation in the brain from uncontrolled flares and uncontrolled exposures to environmental inputs, this can lead to neuropsychological and neurobehavioral problems as well as neurodegenerative patterns that result in disease diagnoses.

Psychopathology and The Immune System

What the Science Has Focused On

Identifying the relationships between autoimmunity and chronic inflammatory disease with psychological, personality and neuropsychiatric disorders is now an important area of research. For many years, it has become clear that several affective and personality disorders are either caused or exacerbated by issues of immune system activity, particularly in the case of autoimmune disorders.

Psychosis and Non-Neurological Autoimmune Disorders

A meta-analysis of 31 studies showed that the presence of psychosis increased the risk for Non-Neurological autoimmune disorders (NNAI) and that NNAI disorders also increased the risk for psychosis (Cullen, 2018). NNAI are autoimmune disorders that affect other systems besides the brain, (e.g., Celiac Disease).

The results of the meta-analysis showed a positive association between psychosis and Celiac, Graves, pernicious anemia, psoriasis and others (ibid, 2018). When you get curious about the relationship between autoimmune disease and psychosis and why this would occur, of course the first thing that stands out is inflammation. There also may be a genetic link between NNAI and psychosis because research shows a strong association between genes that play a role in immune regulation and in schizophrenia (ibid, 2018).

Some researchers have proposed that genetic predisposition plus early environmental factors, e.g.

stressors such as an Adverse Childhood Experiences (ACE) and/or infections, may result in brain vulnerabilities. Later on in puberty, environmental stressors along with hormonal changes may result in problems with neuronal circuits, which may give rise to psychosis (Bergnik et al, 2014).

Other studies from Denmark (which included information from the Danish Psychiatric Register on all 7704 people diagnosed with schizophrenia in Denmark between 1981-1998) reported that those with specific autoimmune diseases had a 45% chance of developing schizophrenia. Some of the autoimmune diseases included Celiac, alopecia areata, thyrotoxicosis, polymyalgia rheumatica and Sjögren's syndrome among others (Eaton, 2006).

Separately, Taiwanese researchers found that 11,000 in-patients with schizophrenia had an increased risk of Celiac disease, Graves' disease, pernicious anemia, psoriasis and more (Chen et al., 2012).

Borderline Personality Disorder and Autoimmune Disease

Another example of autoimmunity and personality disorders in the literature includes a small study in which 40 percent of 15 patients with rheumatoid arthritis met the criteria for Borderline Personality Disorder (BPD). However, the author notes that this association may also be influenced by early developmental trauma (e.g. Adverse Childhood Experiences (ACE)) with its subsequent effects on the immune system (Marcenaro, 1999).

Depression, Anxiety, Inflammation and Autoimmune Disease

Researchers also now believe that an increase in depression and anxiety in patients with autoimmune diseases is due to the direct effect of inflammatory cytokines on the central nervous system (Bagnato, 2006). Increases in inflammatory cytokines from environmental insults (air pollution, noise, food) that lead to glial cell inflammation in the brain, can make matters worse. Glial cells are the sensitive immune cells of the brain that (when inflamed) contribute to neuroinflammation, which may show up as pain, depression, activation of the HPA and hyperarousal of the sympathetic nervous system. The overall inflammatory state can continue chronically if we don't know how to properly halt this influx of inflammation. In all of the above cases, stress and autoimmune-related inflammation may aggravate psychological symptoms and vice versa.

Mitochondria, Inflammation and Translational Psychiatry

Mitochondria are considered the powerhouse of our cells in that they provide the energy needed for normal functioning. It is now thought that our fight-or-flight stress response demands that our mitochondria produce more energy for faster breathing and heart rate to occur. However, mitochondria have slower repair mechanisms, making them vulnerable to damage when acute stress strikes. If any distortion to mitochondrial metabolism occurs, mitochondrial DNA nucleotides (e.g. purines (et al mitokines)) leak out of the cells and trigger immune reactivity. This is referred to as the cell danger response (CDR) (Naviaux, 2012).

It is thought that mitochondrial DNA trigger an immune response due to the fact of mitochondria's bacterial origin. In this scenario immune cells see mitochondrial DNA as a foreign invader. This increases circulating cytokines (messenger immune cells) not only at the site of injury but also in the brain, which leads to neuroinflammation.

Further, animal studies (Gong, 2011) have shown that chronic stress leads to mitochondrial damage in:

- the hippocampus
- the hypothalamus
- the cerebral cortex.

We also now know that psychological stress causes the same cell danger response in humans. In fact, one study showed that floating mitochondrial DNA levels increased significantly (more than double) for 30 minutes after a stressful event. It is now thought that circulating mitochondrial DNA acts like a hormone (Picard, 2018). In the same way as adrenal glands release cortisol in response to stress, circulating mitochondrial DNA is also triggered by stress.

The field of Translational Psychiatry is known for applying clinical findings in neuroscience with novel treatment concepts. The Translational Psychiatry model has been looking at the fact that elevated levels of mitochondrial DNA outside the cell is not only a hallmark of the stress response but very common in those with major depression who are not responding to antidepressant medication. In the emerging research on mitochondrial DNA, scientists are recognizing that mitochondria also have effects on autism spectrum disorders, schizophrenia, Alzheimer's, arthritis and cancer—all problems where inflammation is rampant.

Psychological trauma, particularly Adverse Childhood Experiences (ACE), can also activate the cell danger response, produce chronic inflammation, and increase the risk of many disorders (Ehlers, 2013). The cell danger response can persist when we are constantly exposed to pathogens, trauma et al stressors. The goal of therapy is to resolve the cell danger response to allow healing to occur. Of course the first task is to find and resolve the root causes that are driving the persistent cell danger response, then to use therapeutic agents and interventions to restore homeostasis.

As we start to realize the effects of chronic inflammation and autoimmune disease going forward, we will consider strategies to help to clear a cell danger response that has been kept active by constant resignaling of danger from viruses, bacteria, PTSD or other triggering or traumatic events. See "Upping Your Adaptive Strategy" below for ways to support your mitochondria.

This new understanding of circulating mitochondrial DNA demonstrates how psychological stress may enhance the inflammatory state of the brain-body, which leads to psychological, neurological or immune-mediated disorders involving inflammation.

Neurological Autoimmunity and Neuroinflammation

With the explosion of autoimmune diseases, it has also come to light that autoimmunity and inflammation may play a pathogenic role in symptoms very similar to Alzheimer's disease, which is considered a neurodegenerative disorder. This is now termed neurological autoimmunity.

Neurological autoimmunity can involve any part of the nervous system and can cause weakness, poor brain function, dizziness, tingling sensations in the hands and feet, obsessive-compulsive disorder, nausea, car or seasickness, poor balance, anxiety, and sound and light hypersensitivity. If you have these symptoms, plus significant memory loss and/or vertigo, and you are not a geriatric patient, it's a red flag for early neurological autoimmunity.

Neurological autoimmunity includes multiple sclerosis, neuromyelitis, autoimmune neuropathy, paraneoplastic syndrome and stiff person syndrome. Symptoms of the common neurological tissue antibody autoimmunity, e.g., to the cerebellum, will result in poor balance, movement induced nausea, dizziness, motion sickness, carsickness, seasickness, and sporadic ataxia.

If there's any accelerated brain degeneration, and the person has an autoimmune disease, it is important for practitioners to check for neurological autoimmunity. This includes doing serum tissue antibody testing for myelin basic protein, GAD antibodies, cerebellar antibodies, synapsin antibodies, alpha and beta tubulin antibodies, and asialoganglioside antibodies. You can check GAD antibodies specifically for sporadic ataxia. You can also check myelin basic antibodies, which show up as diverse neurological symptoms and/or idiopathic neuropathy.

We also now know that cerebellar antibodies are cross-reactive with gluten, so it's important to avoid gluten in general, and especially if you have the signs of cerebellar antibodies, plus anxiety, obsessive compulsive disorder, sound and light hypersensitivity, hypokinetic movement disorders or stiff person syndrome.

Based on immunologic dysregulation, the neurological autoimmunity model suggests that antibrain antibodies may contribute to neuroinflammation and neurodegeneration, which present similarly to Alzheimer's disease. But what about the effect of autoimmune inflammation on other comorbid issues (e.g., anxiety that occurs simultaneously) that often exist among those who suffer from autoimmune disease? Does increased inflammation predispose you to experience anxiety and depression, poor mental clarity, anger? The answer is a resounding YES! It absolutely does.

We need to consider this critical information for preventing inflammation from consuming our brain capacity before it's too late. Sure, we need to clean up our gut with an anti-inflammatory diet, balance our hormones, make sure we are detoxing properly and increase oxygenation to the brain. What we have not yet implemented is a way to prevent inflammation from a brain-based perspective.

Personality Neuroscience

Although we traditionally have been taught to study personality at a biological and psychological trait level, we now know that the brain is the source of all human behavior. In recent years, the neurobiological substrates of personality have been explored by looking at brain structure and function, which is considered the premier backdrop of behavioral expression. Identifying the neural mechanisms that underlie differences in personality, along with environmental and cultural influences, has been the focus of the emerging field of personality neuroscience.

Healthy brain structure and function is supported by white matter projections that form what is known as the human connectome. It is now thought that differences in brain connectivity may explain part of the variation in personalities. In fact, studies show that distinct white matter pathways within the striatum (located in the basal ganglia) appear to differentially predict the traits of novelty seeking and reward dependence (Cohen et al., 2009), with tract strength between the ventral striatum and amygdala correlating positively with novelty seeking, and tract strength between striatal and frontal regions correlating positively with reward dependence.

Personality Types and Disease Risk

A personality type is a collection of traits that make up a general personality classification. Personality types represent cognitive, emotional, sensory and behavioral preferences of the so-called "developed self" i.e. all of the neural pathways that we have burned into our brains up until this very moment. The risk of developing certain diseases has been associated with human personality types throughout the history of medicine. Examples include the 5 Element personality types in Traditional Chinese Medicine and Hippocrates' four types of temperament.

More recently, since the mid 1970's, Type A personality traits such as aggression, competitiveness and obsessionality have been correlated with coronary heart disease, allergies and autoimmune disease. Type C, originally considered the cancer personality type that tends toward emotional repression and inability to express anger, is now also correlated with rheumatoid arthritis, multiple sclerosis, systemic lupus erythematosus and other autoimmune disorders (Mate, 2003). Type D personality, sometimes referred to as the distressed or depressed type, has been correlated with autoimmune diseases such as ulcerative colitis (Marzieh et al, 2012) rheumatoid arthritis (Klaassen, 2012) and multiple sclerosis (Seden, 2016).

There may yet be a new personality type to discover that is based on gifted personality traits such as enhanced cognitive capacity, high sensitivity and rumination (Karpinski, 2017). For all of the gifted people of the world, as well as for geeks and other highly creative people, we can now call this Type G. Type G's have heightened neural circuitry which makes them prone to anxiety, depression, ADHD, sensory processing sensitivity, food and environmental sensitivities as well as autoimmune disease.

While much of the research on personality type related to autoimmune disease has focused on traits and coping styles, in this book we will also consider the dominant brain networks and underlying neurobiological needs that may be contributing to autoimmune reactions.

Not everyone fits into a particular type. In fact, as you read through the descriptions, you may notice that you identify with more than one type. The key point is to pay attention to the brain networks and neurobiological needs involved in each type. Let's start with Type A.

Type A Personality

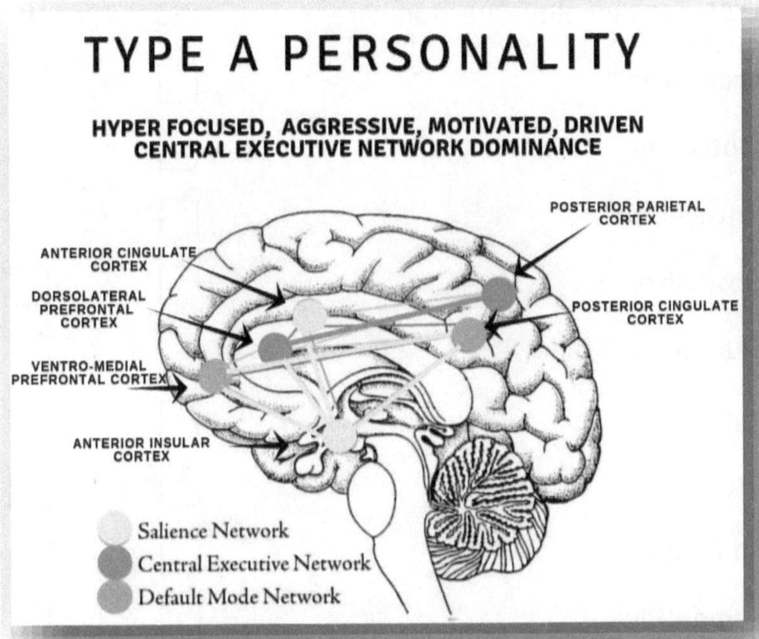

Please fill out the following questionnaire to see if this applies to you.

TYPE A Personality Questionnaire	YES	NO
Aggressive	☐	☐
Motivated	☐	☐
Extraverted	☐	☐
Obsessive	☐	☐
Blunt and/or rude	☐	☐
Impatient	☐	☐
Driven	☐	☐
Ambitious	☐	☐
Competitive	☐	☐
Perfectionist	☐	☐
Workaholic	☐	☐
Easily angered	☐	☐
Stressed and anxious	☐	☐
Unhealthy dependence on external rewards such as wealth, status or power	☐	☐

TYPE A PERSONALITY TRAITS

Aggressive

Impatient

Short tempered

Blunt and/or rude

Motivated

Driven

Ambitious

Competitive

Perfectionist

Workaholic

Easily angered

Stressed and anxious

Unhealthy dependence on external rewards

Type A and The Executive Self

Type A's are generally extraverts who don't waste time. They are also motivated perfectionists who are prone to worry. They are extremely efficient and center their life on their careers but tend to be workaholics. They find it hard to relax and feel most comfortable when working and getting things done.

In terms of brain networks, Type A's are Central Executive Network (CEN) dominant. This brain circuitry is most closely associated with our "executive self," which is involved in sustained attention, working memory, making decisions and initiating actions. This is what drives left brain dominance.

Type A's may become impatient with delays and schedule too many commitments. Because of this, Type A individuals are easily 'wound up' and tend to overreact, have high blood pressure (hypertension) and are easily aroused to anger or hostility, which they may or may not express overtly. As a result, they are more likely to have an increase in stress hormones, which further leads to inflammation and stress-related illnesses. In fact, Type A personality traits may make them more prone to CHD, raised blood pressure, anxiety, allergies and autoimmune reactions. From a hemispheric balance perspective, one can imagine a left-brain in overdrive combined with a weak right hemisphere that can neither regulate emotions nor integrate sensory experiences.

In the case of Type A personality, the degree of reactivity of the nervous system to the stress of chronic extraversion, competition and aggression, determines reactions not only in the cardiovascular system, but also in the immune system. These reactions are mediated by the neuroendocrine system (hypothalamic–pituitary–adrenal (HPA) axis).

In behavioral models, coping styles to acute and chronic stress play an important role in the neuroendocrine system response. For example those with active coping styles (Type A's) produce catecholamines (e.g. adrenaline) in response to acute stress while chronic stress in Type A's tends to activate the HPA, increase ACTH and lower immunity. This response is part of what makes Type A's prone to coronary heart disease, allergies and autoimmune disease.

Type A, The Ego and Rumination

Being worriers, Type A's may get caught in rumination and negative thinking if they aren't careful. On a neuropsychological level, the ego is represented by the default mode network (DMN), which is active when our mind is wandering, e.g., when we are thinking about our self and others, remembering the past or imagining the future. On a neurobiological level, excessive functioning of the DMN creates hyper-plasticity and hyper-functionality.

This not only alters your perceptions and cognitive functions but also may engage the HPA and the amygdala and keep you in chronic stress and rumination mode. When we find ourselves repeatedly responding to internal and external triggers, this self-reinforcing loop may be keeping the hypothalamus and pituitary churning out neurotransmitters and hormones that match our negative emotions and further intensifying the limbic–neural nets, increasing the alarm/stress response.

If we are stuck in ruminative neural networks, there may be less activity in other regions of the brain that aid in logic, intuition and metacognition, namely, the prefrontal regions required for better top down control over our runaway thoughts and elaborate egoic stories.

Type A's and Reward Deficiency

Another consequence of highly motivated Type A's is that they may suffer from reward deficiency, as all the winning, food and social status in the world may not yield satisfactory results. While this keeps Type A's motivated constantly, if their reward seeking needs go unmet, they may default into a state of frustration, clinging and grasping. Interestingly, altered functional and structural organization of the DMN may be the underlying neurobiological feature of anger, aggression and reward seeking behaviors.

In this case you can support the brain in the following ways:

1. Practice neuroplastic techniques like meditation, breathing, aromatherapy with lavender, bergamot and citrus essential oils.
2. Natural ways to increase serotonin and dopamine, include exercise, clean diet, and a combination of dietary supplements, such as Serotone and Dopatone
3. Music for reward - builds expectation delight and surprise, may prompt dopamine/serotonin reward centers to seal in more functionally connected neural networks.

Type C Personality

The Type C personality exhibits traits related to introversion and neuroticism, which are typical of a passive coping style. In the case of Type C, this generally shows up as emotional repression and boundary confusion.

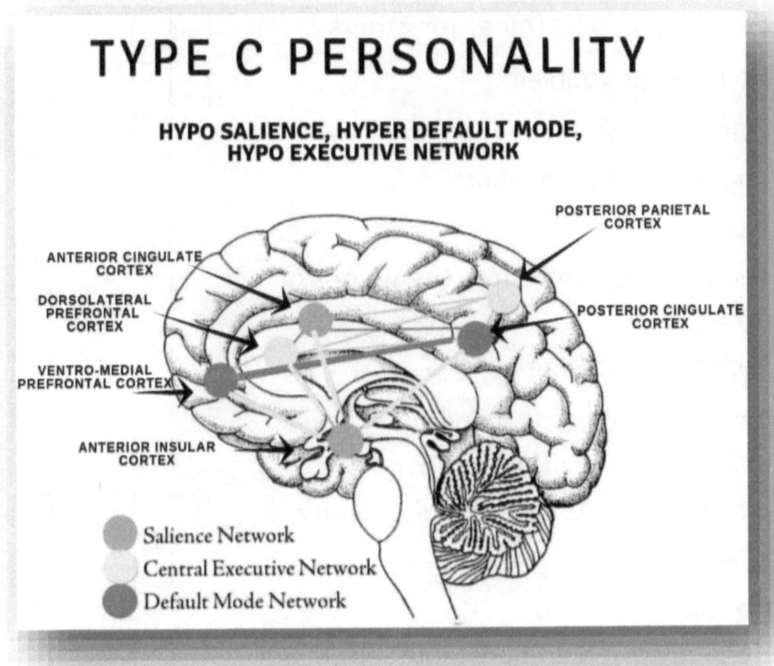

Please fill out the following questionnaire to see if this applies to you.

TYPE C Personality Questionnaire	YES	NO
Emotionally repressed	☐	☐
Ignores or suppresses significant feelings	☐	☐
Unable to express anger	☐	☐
Inability to recognize your own needs	☐	☐
Constantly doing things for others	☐	☐
No time for yourself	☐	☐
Calm, outwardly rational, and unemotional demeanor	☐	☐
Agreeable	☐	☐
Tendency to conform to the wishes of others	☐	☐
Lack of assertiveness	☐	☐
Inclination toward feelings of helplessness or hopelessness	☐	☐
Inability to defend personal integrity	☐	☐
Tends to be codependent and has trouble saying "no"	☐	☐
Has a distorted and unstable self-image or sense of self	☐	☐
Introverted – recharges with alone time	☐	☐
Passive – to avoid conflict	☐	☐
Excessive kindness	☐	☐
Unobtrusiveness	☐	☐
Self-depreciation	☐	☐
Perfectionist	☐	☐

TYPE C PERSONALITY TRAITS

Emotionally Repressed

Unable to express anger

Lack of assertiveness

Feelings of helplessness or hopelessness

Inability to defend personal integrity

Boundary Confusion

Passive - to avoid conflict

Excessive kindness

Codependency

Always puts others first

Type C- Emotional Repression

Type C's have difficulty expressing emotions, particularly negative ones such as anger. This means that this type tends to avoid conflict, ignore their own important feelings and put others' needs before their own. Some psychologists suggest that because Type C individuals deny their feelings, they cannot stand up for themselves, they can't defend their own personal integrity and have trouble saying no and setting boundaries.

It is thought that in suppressing emotions and putting others first, the immune system responds by attacking versus defending the self. If you tend to lack boundaries and are emotionally porous, your immune system will reflect this back to you by way of an illness - be it an infection, cancer or autoimmune reactions.

When not in touch with their emotions, Type C's may be at the effect of unintegrated emotional experiences that can get sublimated in the body. Those with low self-esteem and a poor sense of boundaries may also have increased activity in the default mode network (DMN), that may lead them to getting stuck in negative thoughts.

Studies have shown that changes in key nodes of the brain's default mode network (DMN) may contribute to atypical integration of information about the self in relation to 'other,' which may also impair the ability to relate to others socially. The neurobiological landscape includes a hypofunctioning prefrontal cortex and an inability to self-reflect and/or be astute to their own emotions and the emotions of others.

Perhaps constricted self-expression is due to not knowing how to develop functional connectivity in the brain. Self-reflection and introspection may also not be in the cards if the person's brain also has a deficit in certain structures (and attendant lack of functional flow), namely, the anterior insular cortex and the prefrontal cortex. The anterior insular cortex is one of the key nodes of the salience network, which is involved in self-awareness and emotional responsiveness. The prefrontal cortex is involved in self-reflection, evaluating and initiating approach behaviors, decision-making, reasoning and analytic thinking.

Type C – Boundary Confusion

Type C personalities exhibit a passive coping style, which may not serve them well in stressful situations. Those with a passive coping style (e.g. Type C) exhibit activation of the HPA in response to acute stress (as demonstrated by high levels of ACTH (adrenocorticotropic hormone)), which is then followed by adrenal exhaustion as measured by low cortisol (Frank et al, 2006).

One a cellular level, the passive coping style of Type C's to acute stress is associated with decreased monocyte numbers and a decrease in T-helper lymphocytes (Sakami et al., 2004). High introversion and high neuroticism (which is typical of passive coping styles), is also associated with low IFN (interferon) production by blood lymphocytes (Surkina et al, 2001). All of these markers point toward lowered immune defenses and vulnerability to invasion by pathogens et al pernicious influences from the environment. On a psychological level this may show up as boundary invasion by others and not being able to defend your personal integrity. In fact, autoimmune disease has also been associated with Type C passive coping tendencies of emotional repression and boundary confusion (Mate, 2003).

When cognitive capacity is impaired by inflammation on top of neurobiological deficits, this shows up as cognitive problems. This would indicate hypofunctioning in the prefrontal cortex and perhaps working memory within the hippocampus being impaired by stress. If the functional connectivity among these brain regions is decreased, cognitive issues may arise. This may present with brain fog, inability to concentrate, forgetfulness and mental fatigue.

When disconnected areas of the brain rule, your cognitive, emotional and behavioral styles may express as being inattentive, brain fogged, forgetful and dull. All of this can lead to an inability to do 'self-referential processing.' This refers to the ability to process social information relative to oneself and the ability to understand the beliefs, intentions and emotions of others. This can set you up for boundary confusion.

Because they tend to conform to the wishes of others, Type C personalities may unconsciously fall into the trap of getting caught up in codependency and toxic reward loops. They may have unexamined and/or unconscious beliefs about how they go about getting their needs met. If there is also a hypofunctioning of the prefrontal cortex and/or decreased gray matter in the insular cortex, they will fail to gain insight into their toxic attachment styles and may therefore remain in codependent relationships.

If Type C's do not get to the root cause (i.e., their own neurobiological deficits), they may never learn how to break free of toxic reward patterning and the neuroplasticity required to improve brain function.

To take away the negative spin, we can also look at it as a means to learning what areas are screaming out for neuroplastic techniques. Areas to target in the brain itself would be the prefrontal cortex (specifically the orbitofrontal cortex (OFC)), as well as the salience network (SN) and the default mode network (DMN). Meditation, a good sense of humor and prayer will help wake up the OFC and shift you out of the negativity bias of the default network (DMN) while body scanning, interoception and self-massage will improve connectivity within the salience network.

Interventions

- Check neurotransmitter imbalance and need for nutritional neuroplasticity: e.g., acetylcholine for the PFC
- Support the PFC with exercise
- Implement interoception techniques such as mindful body scanning
- Practice naming your emotions and allowing time for integration
- Add music, sound and essential oils, e.g., pine for mental clarity
- Anti-inflammatory diet
- Meditation and prayer
- Humor and laughter
- Massage

Type D Personality - Distressed

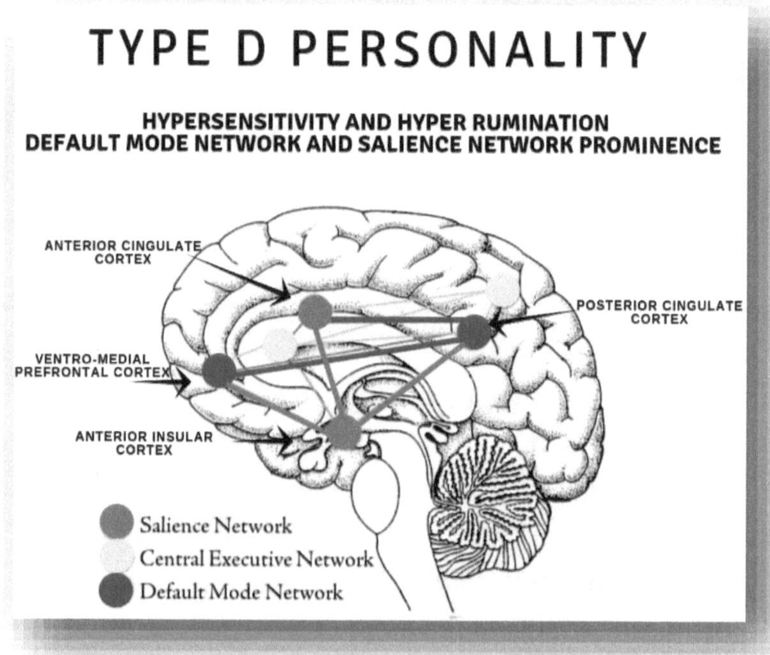

Please fill out the following questionnaire to see if this applies to you.

TYPE D Personality Questionnaire	YES	NO
Negative view about self	☐	☐
Shyness, fear in groups	☐	☐
Fear of embarrassment	☐	☐
Fear of failure, perfectionism	☐	☐
Feel like you don't fit in	☐	☐
Difficulty understanding social situations	☐	☐
Has feelings of isolation	☐	☐
Difficulty understanding others' thoughts and feelings	☐	☐
Feels as if missing the conversation gene	☐	☐
Poor eye contact	☐	☐
Inhibits emotions in social interactions	☐	☐
Difficulty making friendships	☐	☐
Avoids expressing negative emotions in social situations	☐	☐
Fear of social disapproval	☐	☐
On constant lookout for danger – vigilant	☐	☐
Underlying anxiety or negativity	☐	☐
Insecure; low self-esteem	☐	☐
Depressed	☐	☐
Constant feelings of overwhelm	☐	☐
Angry	☐	☐
Irritable	☐	☐
Prone to fear, disgust, anxiety and worry	☐	☐
Harm avoidant – prefers activities that are safe	☐	☐
History of traumatic event in early childhood	☐	☐
Feelings of a "knot" in your stomach	☐	☐
Startles easily	☐	☐
Dysphoric mood	☐	☐

TYPE D PERSONALITY TRAITS

Negative Affectivity:
The tendency to experience negative emotions across various times and situations, neuroticism, dysphoria, worry, anxiety, depression, irritability, anger and a negative view about self and the external world.

Social Inhibition:
Inhibition of emotions in social interactions.
Fear of disapproval or getting no reward from others.

TYPE D Personalities and Autoimmune Disease

Type D personality has been suggested in the literature in the past twenty years. The two main traits associated with Type D's include Negative Affectivity (NA) and Social Inhibition (SI). Negative affectivity refers to the tendency to experience negative emotions across time, and is closely is related to neuroticism.

In Sigmund Freud's theory of psychoanalysis, the term neurotic is used as a label for symptoms that are related to psychological disturbances. High scores in neuroticism are associated with feelings of dysphoria, worry, anxiety, depression, irritability, anger and a negative view about self and the external world. Neuroticism is also related to a hyperfunctioning brain network called the default mode network (DMN).

Social inhibition or shyness in groups and a tendency to inhibit the expression of emotions in social interactions is common in Type D personalities. They may feel as if they are missing the conversation gene and prefer social isolation to avoid disapproval from others. Since the type D personality generally has a negative view of life and tends to suppress their emotions in social situations, they are also highly susceptible to depression. They may have low self-esteem and fear of rejection and are often stressed, angry, worried and tense. They are generally imagining and waiting for the worst to happen. Type D's are constantly searching for security and reward from the outside world but never seem to feel safe or satisfied.

Interestingly, people who lack gray matter volume in specific brain structures involved in self-other relating (e.g., the mirror neuron system and the insular cortex) are generally lacking in self-referential and social communication skills. That is, they may have trouble introspecting and also might shy away from social interaction. This is a major clue to a right brain imbalance.

The right brain is about reading people and situations. If you never fully developed nonverbal skills (reading others' emotions), it may make socializing with others difficult. When you don't get that feedback, it's hard to read your own emotions and the problem continues due to a lack of plasticity that needs to be restored. If you notice being disconnected to your own emotions, start your intervention on the key brain areas involved to maximize plasticity and improve functional connectivity. For example, you can practice naming your emotions and doing some body scanning techniques to build up the insular cortex.

The insula (along with the ACC, vmPFC and orbitofrontal cortex (OFC)), serves as a conduit for the flow of information that allows us to form pictures of the state of our own bodies and of one another's minds. This is referred to as theory of mind (ToM). Deficits in this function are referred to as mind-blindness.

It also helps to understand the emotional brain and the underlying biological needs that are beneath our personality tendencies. The basic emotions include happiness, sadness, anger/hostility, fear, shame and guilt. The limbic (emotional) brain is approximately 100 million years old. Most people in general walk around with a "hot" limbic system that creates a lot of inflammation when we perseverate in negative emotional states. It is well documented that hostility, anger and shame increase pro-inflammatory cytokines like IL1, IL2, IL6 and TNF-alpha (Dickerson, 2004, Suarez, 2012). Whether it's being resentful or angry about the past, fearing something in the future or feeling shame about something, these states lead to inflammation and immune imbalance.

Indeed, some authors have suggested that Type D personalities are associated with greater cortisol reactivity to stress and increased level of Tumor Necrosis Factor (TNF) resulting from an immune dysregulation response from autoimmune disease itself. This cytokine shift towards greater inflammation impacts brain structures in the limbic system related to negative affect and social inhibition. That is, the HPA likely gets agitated and feeds into aberrant salience and default network looping.

When we're polarized in emotional or physical stresses, we stay locked in high sympathetic tone, low parasympathetic tone and a high level of stress hormones like cortisol. High levels of cortisol may directly destroy cells in the hippocampus, which is the brain's memory center. Since high levels of cortisol also lead to more immune-system imbalance and accelerated brain aging, it is important to intervene and have a plan to reduce your exposure to anything that stresses you out.

Besides being involved in the encoding of new memories, the hippocampus helps us control our emotional response by transforming sensory stimuli into hormonal signals. These signals send information to other parts of the brain that control behavior. When we perceive a threat, our hippocampus compares it to previous unconscious dangers. The hippocampus then communicates to our amygdala by sending alerts to the fight-or-flight and hormonal systems.

When we are stuck in the sympathetic fight-flight-freeze response, it's imperative to leverage every possible modality to kick in the parasympathetic rest and digest response. When the sympathetic nervous system is dominant, symptoms of high stress, poor digestion, poor sleep, increased heart rate, inappropriate temperature regulation and dizziness when standing up quickly, may start showing up.

Depression, Anger and Negative Emotions

From a neurobiological standpoint, negative emotions like anger and depression stem from basic needs for satisfaction and safety going unmet. This is also a clue that certain brain areas are screaming out for proper balance – namely, the safety and reward centers.

Aggressive behavior, depression and negative emotions have to do with specific areas of the brain that you need to know how to work with if you choose to recover and restore your brain. Structural brain areas to target for anger, depression and negative emotions include the prefrontal cortex (PFC), the amygdala and the hippocampus.

Having a hypofunctioning PFC means having a more difficult time with emotional regulation. The PFC is what regulates the amygdala and the rest of the limbic/emotional brain. The untamed amygdala is a constant for anyone who experiences chronic overwhelming emotional responses. It is thought that unconscious emotional memories in the amygdala are the seat of anxiety disorders.

When there is increased activity in the amygdala, finding a way to reduce it is critical to recovering from the neurally programmed emotional looping. This may mean addressing unconscious fear memories along with supporting the prefrontal cortex (PFC). To support the PFC, we start by reducing anything that's inflaming it - including autoimmune disease, foods, chemicals, air and people. Familiarizing yourself with the amygdala's gatekeepers - the anterior cingulated cortex (ACC), the dorsolateral prefrontal cortex (DLPFC), the insular cortex and the basal ganglia - will also help you navigate overwhelming emotional reactions.

Since the right hemisphere has to do with regulating the immune system as well as integrating the senses and emotions, any problems that arise can be looked at as lack of plasticity in related brain areas. For example, in the case of autoimmune disease, we can address sensory and emotional structures in the brain. This can be a pure application of neuroscience in the clinical setting or at home.

Handling Depression, Anger and Negative Emotions

Those with chronic negative emotions may experience mood swings, poor impulse control, volatile emotions and failure to form normal personal relationships. The field of Psycho-Neuro-immunology (PNI) studies the interface of the immune system with the brain and emotions. We now know that parts of the immune system may generate systemic responses to certain emotions. When we get stuck in unhealthy emotional states, immune mediators, such as cytokines, chemokines and free radicals, may cause tissue damage leading to chronic inflammation. If negative emotions are not recognized or dealt with, over time this can increase the risk of neurobiological deficits and brain degeneration. Other factors, including genetic mutations and environmental exposure, may also have an effect on emotions and personality, which in turn affect immune activity.

The default mode network (DMN) of the brain is likely the prime suspect in terms of negative emotions and rumination and will need to be deactivated through top down skills gained via various meditation and mindfulness techniques.

For example, it has been shown that the wiring between the prefrontal cortex and the limbic brain, or the white matter structures, can be more functionally connected and organized as a result of practices such as meditation and mindfulness. These practices break up the DMN and give the brain something to do in terms of shutting down the structures that would normally be off in mind wandering, and now are being directed to look inward. If the brain is caught up in the DMN and emotional fear based structures – namely the amygdala - it may be hard to break these loops because you don't even know you're in them.

Once you stem the tide of mental looping, try to understand and calm down any fear that is driving the loop. First, figure out the needs behind the fear (hint: safety, comfort and security). Then, get grounded by engaging in activities that calm down the sympathetic nervous system and restore the parasympathetic rest-digest-healing mode. This will kick in vagal toning and is achievable with exercise, yoga, breathing, massage, acupuncture, music and any interoceptive (body and organ scanning) and exteroceptive techniques like Tai Qi and Qi Gong, which are neuroplastic techniques.

It's also important to prioritize alone time to process your sensations and feelings, to exercise and get enough sleep and to reach out to a trusted friend or therapist about what you're going through. When you can identify where you are stuck in negative thoughts, you can also correct your misperceptions with mindfulness, equanimity and reframing.

Mindfulness, Equanimity and Reframing

Conventional and alternative treatments for anger, depression and negative emotions usually include medications and herbal remedies. Other research shows that you can benefit from neuroplastic techniques like meditation and mindfulness. The more in control of your perceptions and reactions, the more wisdom, peace and confidence you will feel. Investigating the root cause and needs behind negative emotions will increase your self-awareness of where your mind gets caught in neural grooves. Introspection is key - look into yourself, not for the purpose of judgment, but to improve your reactions and interpretation of events and circumstances.

Remember to simply view anything appearing off balance or abnormal in the associative (cognitive- thought), feeling (limbic) and behavioral (psychomotor) realms as likely having to do with a hemispheric imbalance upstream. Observe and work with the pattern until extinction learning is complete. In whatever ways possible – including talking to a therapist, to your inner child or to animals, you entrain a conscious effort to improve your ability to integrate cognitive, sensory and emotional data. You are literally improving functional connectivity in real time.

We sometimes can acknowledge that we are stuck in unconscious memories when our behavior appears irrational to us. But we haven't been taught how to skillfully, sensitively and ethically escort these unconscious fears to the light and to conscious reappraisal of how it's fuelling inflammatory physiology.

There is a way. We can use neuroplastic techniques as needed to keep our brain nourished. For example, cortical and subcortical techniques such as Emo-Sensory Therapy can introduce pleasant sensory experiences and attendant positive emotions (and neurotransmitters) that go along with getting our needs met. In this way, you intentionally lay down new brain pathways and are now in more control of your neural nets. Consider it a sonic dose of GABA, dopamine, serotonin and oxytocin to satisfy the basic neurobiological needs of the brain, namely, safety, satisfaction-reward, happiness, acceptance and belonging. This calms inflammatory genes and regulates immune function.

Type D's and Reward Deficiency

Since Type D's also suffer from reward deficiency, you can support the brain in the following ways:

1. Practice neuroplastic techniques like meditation, breathing, aromatherapy with citrus essential oils.

2. Find natural ways to increase serotonin and dopamine, include exercise, clean diet, and a

combination of dietary supplements, such as Serotone and Dopatone

3. Music for reward - builds expectation, delight and surprise, may prompt dopamine/serotonin reward centers to seal in more functionally connected neural networks.

Type G Personality

Any comprehensive understanding of autoimmune personality traits must take into account, gifted intelligence. It turns out that those with high IQ may be more prone to not only anxiety and depression but also to autoimmune disease and sensory processing sensitivities. In fact, the literature is filled with examples of highly intelligent people suffering many physiological responses as a result of heightened neural circuitry in the brain (Karpinski, 2017).

After investigating personality types for my book, <u>Gifted Intelligence</u>, I propose that people with autoimmune disease fall into several types - one of which includes gifted traits, that I have termed Type G. The term gifted refers to an ability to sense, perceive and interpret the world in a quicker and more detailed manner than the bulk of the population.

The research showed that giftedness was related to sensory processing sensitivity, autoimmunity, ADHD, autism spectrum and affective disorders. This piqued my curiosity and I started looking into the brain networks related to gifted intelligence.

Across-the-board, it seemed like the three main brain networks that are involved in gifted tendencies make up a mosaic of personality traits, including enhanced cognitive capacity, high sensitivity and tendency toward rumination. Because these traits are mainly attributed to those with gifted intelligence, we could easily term this Type G personality, which stands for gifted or geek personality.

The main overlap of studied traits that seem to correspond to physiological responses in the body have to do with hypersensitivity or sensory processing hypersensitivities (the salience network), hyper rumination disorders, such as anxiety and depression or negative affect (the default mode network), and the central executive network (CEN), which has to do with the rational "executive" self that, in the case of the gifted, is hell-bent on higher knowledge, wisdom, justice and the search for truth.

The overengagement of these three networks with hyper focus, hyper salience and hyper rumination, plus chronic activation of the hypothalamic pituitary adrenal (HPA) axis, likely keeps autoimmune symptoms flaring. In other words, Type G's are more susceptible to anxiety, depression, OCD, ADHD, allergies and autoimmune reactions due to highly charged neural circuitry in the brain, activation of the HPA and concomitant hypersensitivity.

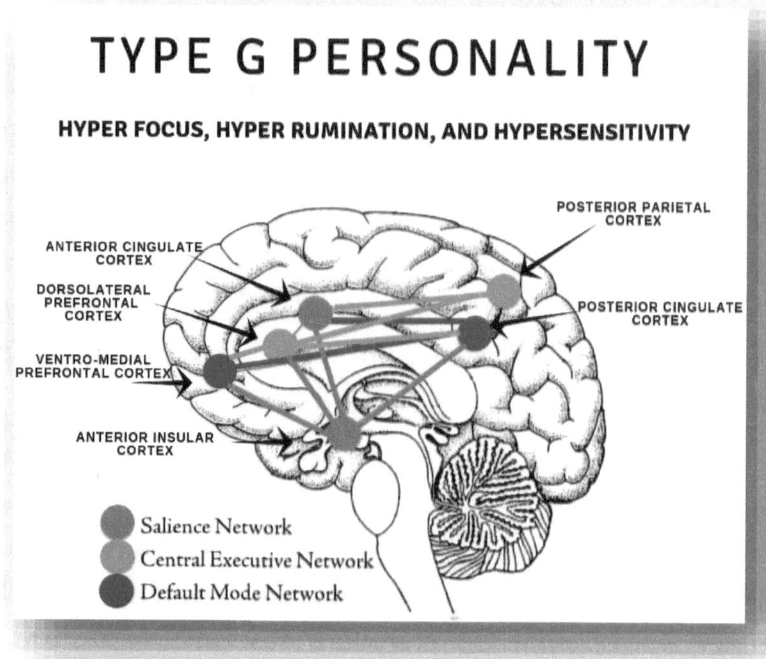

Please fill out this questionnaire to see if this applies to you.

TYPE G Personality Questionnaire	YES	NO
Very curious and freely approaches new situations	☐	☐
Highly verbal	☐	☐
Analytical thinker	☐	☐
Good at memorizing large amounts of data	☐	☐
Avid reader	☐	☐
Searches for truth, justice and understanding	☐	☐

Conscientious	☐	☐
Love of problem solving	☐	☐
Motivated by ideas	☐	☐
Fidgety, can't sit still	☐	☐
Inability to handle stress – easily overwhelmed	☐	☐
Identifies with the feelings of others	☐	☐
Empathic	☐	☐
Anxiety	☐	☐
Depression	☐	☐
Painfully sensitive to criticism	☐	☐
Physical response to emotions (stomach aches, headaches)	☐	☐
Easily bothered by noise, lights and smells	☐	☐
Very perceptive and insightful	☐	☐
Struggles with mood swings	☐	☐
Requires a large amount of downtime	☐	☐
Highly intuitive to others' feelings	☐	☐
Thin skinned or feels emotionally porous	☐	☐
Startles easily	☐	☐
Sensitive to perfumes, foods, alcohol, etc.	☐	☐
Avoids negative and/or violent movies	☐	☐
Experiences sensory overload	☐	☐
Easily overwhelmed at parties or in large crowds	☐	☐
Perfectionist	☐	☐

The Top 3 Traits That May be Predisposing You to Flares:

Enhanced Cognitive Capacity, High Sensitivity, High Rumination

In order to fully understand our personality, we also need to learn how to backtrack from whatever phenotype expression is occurring, to what's going on in the brain. In autoimmune disease, you may have an imbalanced brain in that you have heightened left brain processing abilities and inadequate sensory processing and emotional and immune regulation on the right. This may express as the following gifted personality traits.

TYPE G PERSONALITY TRAITS

High cognitive capacity:
heightened sense of justice,
strong working memory,
rapid information processing
and verbal skills.

High sensitivity:
to environmental stressors, crowds,
other people's emotions,
food, light, sound and scents

High Rumination:
general neuroticism, worry and focus on negative
emotions, anxiety, depression,
poor self regard, fear of disapproval

Brain Networks

In order to understand what's going on in the autoimmune brain, we first need to consider the predominant brain networks that we typically use on a daily basis. For example, the central executive network (CEN) is used for sustained attention, working memory and monitoring goal-directed behavior. The CEN is comprised of the dorsolateral prefrontal cortex (DLPFC) and the posterior parietal cortex (PPC) and activates when we need to focus or control our thought processes.

The default mode network (DMN) is the brain network that processes self-referencing information. The DMN is active when thoughts are directed towards internal processes like idea generation, mind wandering, daydreaming and imagining. The DMN deactivates during processing of external stimuli, e.g., cognitive tasks which activate the CEN instead. The salience network (SN) is responsible for alternating between idea generation (DMN) and idea evaluation (CEN).

High cognitive capacity represents a hyperconnected left brain. High sensitivity and high rumination represent a weak right hemisphere. Besides a dysfunctional posterior cingulate (which is usually in overdrive in the case of rumination), chances are there are also hypoconnected areas of the PFC to the amygdala that exert top down control over the limbic regions. If not corrected, negative hyperplasticity and resultant negative moods stay entrenched in our psyche.

One thing we have not done is examine autoimmune disease from the level of the physical body proper. That is, we need to start considering sensory processing and emotions as unintegrated experiences, which may be due to a lack of functional connectivity from the prefrontal cortex to the sensory and emotional integration areas of the brain. This then reflects in both the brain and body as symptoms.

Therefore, the processing of sensory and emotional experiences is altered and unintegrated until finally dealt with. In a similar way to how we have been managing sensory processing and learning disorders, we can also apply to immune dysfunction and autoimmune disease the remedy of building up the hemispheres of the brain and facilitating emotional and sensory integration. The goal is hemispheric balance by supporting emotional and sensory integration as well as cognitive control.

The Consequence of Being Smart

Those with heightened cognitive capacity, or high IQ, have enhanced functional connectivity in the dorsolateral prefrontal cortex (DLPFC) and the posterior parietal cortex (PPC), which are the two major nodes of the Central Executive Network (CEN). This is the network that is involved in sustained attention, working memory, making decisions and initiating actions. This network is also used a great deal by Type A personalities.

However, while other types can be intelligent, they may not have as heightened cognitive capacity and specific abilities and insights like Type G's. Besides heightened cognitive capacity, Type G's generally have a strong working memory, strong verbal skills, rapid information processing, heightened perceptivity, high sensitivity, a high-level of creativity and a heightened sense of justice.

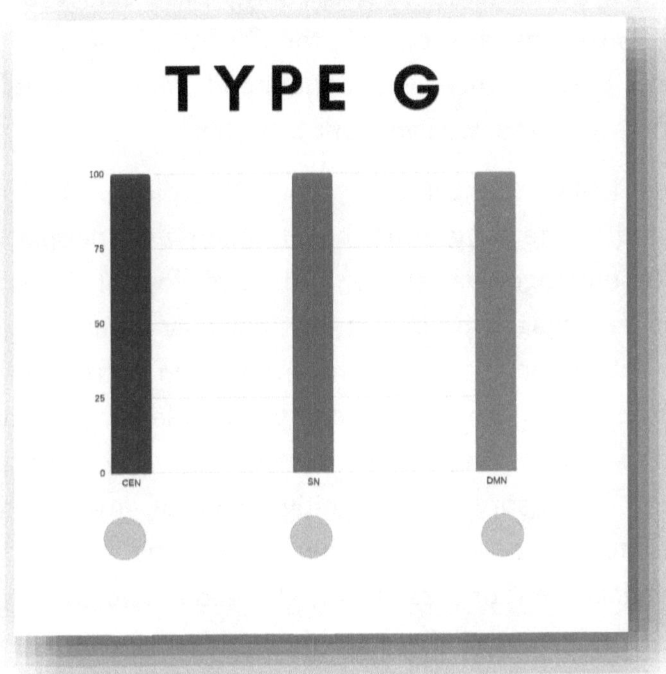

Having a combination of high cognitive capacity, hypersensitivity and rumination contributes to heightened neural circuitry in the brain. Each of these traits relates to the three main brain networks involved in physiological responses: the default mode network (DMN), the salience network (SN) and central executive networks (CEN). The consequences of these traits occur when these networks are overengaged and result in physiological consequences, i.e., a hyper-brain may lead to a hyper-body response.

Said differently, we can consider autoimmune reactions as stemming from over engagement in the three main brain networks: the salience network (SN), DMN and the CEN, along with coactivation of the hypothalamic-pituitary-adrenal (HPA). Once we understand more about the networks involved, we can work with them.

The DMN, the SN and the CEN typically don't get activated at the same time, but it seems as if people with heightened cognitive ability and physiological responses have over engaged brain systems that may be creating too much entropy in the brain. This increase in entropy makes the brain both more creative *and* vulnerable to "blow outs" or flares. Then, the right hemisphere, with decreased emotional, sensory and cognitive control, manifests as autoimmune reactions. In other words, the fallout from over engagement of these highly charged networks is that it can create hyper-reactivity and hyper-plasticity, which may lead to cognitive consequences of hyper-perception, hyper-attention, hyper-memory and hyper-emotionality.

At the end of the day, we need to know that our symptoms can be driven by overly strong reactions to experiences that train the brain into hyper-preferences, which may further be accelerated by emotionally charged experiences and trauma. This perfect storm of brain activity may lead to obsessively detailed information processing, a painfully intense experience of the world and resultant physiological responses. Knowing how to work with each of our highly charged neural nets is imperative for anyone suffering at the effect of hyperplastic networks.

The Ego, the Default Mode Network and Rumination

Type G's may exhibit enhanced perception, memory and attention. This is due to an enhanced affective awareness, which leads to a high perceptivity of the environment. Affective awareness comes from emotional responses to sensory experiences and the meaning created in response to perceptions.

The bottom line is that neurons in the brain may be especially sensitive and flexible in those who have intense perception, hyper-focus, strong memory and strong emotions. This increased activity in neural circuits may allow some people to learn more quickly but may also result in stronger fear responses and stronger fear memories. When rumination is relentless and negative, some may suffer from anxiety and depression, which we now know may drive autoimmune reactions in a vicious cycle.

In the case of rumination, depression, worry and anxiety, the hypothalamic-pituitary-adrenal (HPA) axis, the salience network (SN) and the default mode network (DMN) are all likely at play. It is well known that those who have mood disorders have a hyperactive default mode network (DMN) that stays excitable instead of shutting down. When we are caught up in self-referencing and worried about the past and future, it keeps this cycle going. This may co-activate the salience network, which in turn may create a hyper focus on what is felt and sensed from the negative thought looping of the DMN.

The default mode network is thought to be the neurological basis for the ego. That is, the ego - or the autobiographical self - is generated by the functions of the DMN. The two main nodes of the DMN includes the posterior cingulate cortex (PCC), as well as more frontal regions like the ventro-medial frontal cortex (vmPFC) (Damoiseaux et al., 2006). The default mode network is active when our mind is wandering, e.g., when we are thinking about ourselves and others, remembering the past or imagining the future. This makes for a neurotic mind that has a hard time relaxing the grip of the ego self.

On a neurobiological level, excessive functioning of the DMN creates hyper-plasticity and hyper-functionality. This not only alters your perceptions and cognitive functions but also (especially if incessant and negative) may engage the HPA and the amygdala, as well as the salience network (SN). If we are stuck in ruminative neural networks, there may be less activity in other regions of the brain that aid in logic, intuition and metacognition, namely, the prefrontal regions required for intuitive intelligence.

Further, environmental and psychological threats may prime the HPA to be in a chronic "fight, flight or freeze" response, rendering the nervous system unable to fully relax (Anticevic et al., 2012). In this chronically activated state, the brain stops distinguishing between real and perceived threats and reacts to everything. It's likely that some people with negative affect disorders like rumination and depression feel perceived stressors/threats more intensely than most people due to chronic evaluation of psychological and environmental stressors, made possible by coactivation of the salience network. This combination in turn may further contribute to depression.

Supporting the prefrontal region and these brain networks will yield better top down control over repetitive thoughts and the limbic brain, which in turn will help regulate the body, senses, emotions and social ability.

High Sensitivity and The Salience Network

Many people with autoimmune disease share the same trait of extreme sensitivity – whether it be environmental, emotional or physical. This sensitivity, along with our sense of intuition about what's happening to us, is made possible by the salience network (SN). The SN includes two main nodes: the anterior cingulate cortex (ACC) and the anterior insular cortex (AIC) (Medford et al., 2010). From a neurobiological standpoint, higher levels of awareness and emotional responsiveness in highly sensitive people correlate with greater activity in the anterior insular cortex and mirror neuron areas of the brain.

Even though it's not technically part of the limbic region, the anterior insular cortex acts as a communication relay station between body (via the spinal cord and brainstem), limbic region and cortex. The anterior insular cortex is also involved in interoception, emotional regulation, sudden insight, consciousness, empathy and sense of selfhood. Meanwhile, high activity in the mirror neuron system contributes to enhanced perception of others' movements and intentions.

If the salience and default mode networks over-communicate with each other, our representation of our self may become either more fluid or more chaotic. On the one hand, this can allow more enhanced insight and intuition. On the other hand, the salience network may increase the significance of usually unimportant or negative things. This may be especially true for Type G's who have high sensory processing sensitivities (HSP's) as they tend to have empathic and intuitive personality traits that make them susceptible to social-emotional and environmental stress due to having more permeable boundaries.

Heightened Sensitivity Plus ACE and PTSD

We now know that genes are regulated by environmental signals throughout the course of our development and that early experiences are extremely important in determining long-term individual differences in how these signals will affect brain function, behavior and personality (McEwen, 1999). Because trauma can dramatically impact personality in terms of the way we perceive, sense and feel, it's important to consider what many of us have had to endure in our lifetimes, namely Adverse Childhood Experiences (ACE) and/or post traumatic stress disorder (PTSD).

There is a fair amount of research that correlates Adverse Childhood Experiences (such as emotional neglect, divorce, disruption and trauma, as well as physical and sexual abuse) with autoimmune disease. Examples have included patients with rheumatoid arthritis who report emotional neglect and abuse in their childhood (Walker et al., 1997), patients with systemic lupus erythematosus who reveal marked childhood emotional deprivation (Otto et al., 1967), and MS patients who have poor coping skills that date back to early childhood and correlate positively with symptom severity (Diana et al., 1985).

Persistent stress and inflammation during early childhood is hard to get rid of in part because the brain and central nervous system are still developing. You can imagine that in all of these cases, persistent stress arousal is laying the foundation for later development of physical disease. The takeaway is that chronic stimulation of HPA neurocircuitry, neurohormones and pro-inflammatory cytokines via chronic persistent stress will make you more prone to flare-ups.

Both ACE and PTSD are correlated with an inability to construct a coherent narrative of the past. When people try to speak about traumatic events, you may notice the narrative becoming disorganized and incoherent. It's hard for them to make sense of their own stories.

Think of the left side of brain as the part that does the thinking, while the right side has memories stored as pictures. That is, the language in the right hemisphere is not in the form of words, but in pictures. This is where post-traumatic mental pictures come from. Because there are no words, therapy for people who have PTSD brings in logos/voice/words to make order out of the chaos of trauma. Therapies that stimulate the right hemisphere of the brain include guided imagery, sensate body focusing, body scanning, interoception, Emo-Sensory Therapy and Somatic Experiencing. These therapies all allow for integration of the two hemispheres and are ideal for working with trauma.

We also need to consider the fact that adverse childhood experiences may have a more pervasive impact on sensitive people. Research shows that highly sensitive individuals who endured Adverse Childhood Experiences - or a high degree of stress - are more prone to depression, anxiety or shyness later in life (Aron et al., 2005). Further, sensitive people frequently have over-arousal when trying to express themselves, which contributes to feelings of anxiety and shyness.

Expression of symptoms later in life depends on autoimmune genetic predisposition and the persistence of stressors. Meanwhile, the degree of the stress response determines the degree of neuroendocrine and neuroimmune secretions, which contribute to immune polarization.

Taking Care of The Sensitive Self

To correct immune polarization, we need to coax the body into the relaxation response and decrease the "noise" or immune system interference around us. We need to get grounded in our bodies, where we can pay attention to what we are intending to heal.

The Salience Network (the sensitive and intuitive self) operates in alpha mode, i.e., a slower brain frequency where you can sense and heal yourself. You can enhance this sense of self by stimulating CT (C-Tactile) afferent nerves that carry sensory information from the body to the brain – specifically to the angular gyrus (one of the brain regions which gives us a sense of self) and the insular cortex (one of the main nodes of the salience network, involved in how we sense ourselves internally).

Anything that stimulates the CT afferent nerves will add to the redistribution of communication between networks in the brain. We now know that music, vibration on the skin, heat, cold, therapeutic touch, massage, stretching, acupressure and acupuncture have this effect on these pathways. If we get good at supporting and guiding these networks, neuroplastic strength is bound to follow.

Sensitive Self Support

1. Sound meditation and music

2. Essential oils

3. Acupuncture

4. Massage therapy

5. Restorative yoga and pranayama

6. Anti-inflammatory diet, including Omega-3 EPA/DHA, B Complex and Vitamin D

7. Include natural ways to increase serotonin and GABA with exercise, adequate protein and a combination of dietary supplements, such as Serotone and Gabatone

8. Use music to meet the needs of safety, relaxation, happiness, satisfaction and belonging

9. Emo-Sensory Therapy

The focus is on improving functional connectivity in the regions that need it most. Essentially, it comes down to emotional and sensory integration (aka vertical integration) and getting good at regulating the flow of information from the right to the left brain (aka horizontal integration).

Horizontal Integration - Making the Unconscious Conscious

An integral part of individuation and healing is making what was previously unconscious, conscious. When we confront our unconscious memories, perceptions and beliefs, we need to give consistent comfort and understanding to ourselves for any painful memories that come up. This is the conscious step from the PFC to the limbic amygdala that helps us escort unconscious experiences (from the amygdala) into conscious memory via the hippocampus (where the past is experienced as past).

When your unconscious thoughts, feelings, memories and symptoms start becoming conscious, you start to understand what the origin of the triggered response is. In recognizing the origin of, e.g., your anxiety, you may be able to sit with strong feelings for longer as you steady yourself with compassion and understanding. This kind of right brain repair encourages neural integration that can (with dogged practice) change our mental models and improve immune function.

Other ways to do autotherapy (self-healing) around this issue is to internalize images of calming parental figures who have been absent. Use of gentle and steady binaural beats, Emo-Sensory Therapy and guided meditations can also help escort you on the journey. Increasing self-care leads to increased regulation and healing.

By exposing our tendencies to review by the conscious mind, time expands and we wake up to the experience of being. You now have a front row seat to peer into the theater of your unseen inner landscape. You can even start tracing your emotions, symptoms and behaviors to their source. You can start noticing when your psyche internalizes and acts out emotional needs and behaviors. Then you can start to look behind the trait expression, fear, anger, social awkwardness and sensory processing sensitivities to find meaning. Practicing this will always lead you back to more efficiently understanding yourself. From this more pure vantage point, all of your tendencies can now be viewed as just being human without feeling shame, guilt or inadequacy.

Unconscious Perceptions

The amygdala is the area of the brain that creates nonverbal conclusions about life that serve as mental models of how we perceive the world. These mental models lead to thoughts, ideas and stories that are generally below the level of our conscious awareness. Unfortunately, we may only learn what these unconscious stories are via symptoms or actions that stem from our dominant neural nets. That is, our perceptual biases (mental models) largely come from dominant neural nets that have, up until now, only relied upon a half conscious approach to integration.

When we are emotionally reactive, we need to ask ourselves not only what the underlying need is, but also how we came to believe in and give power to whatever is offensive. Consider having a day of noticing all of your strong reactions, especially your judgments and how much you're cussing out loud or condemning others. You need to realize how you are fulfilling your amygdala's destiny, which is primed to ping at the slightest perception of fear. Since it's such a dominant neural net, you barely notice, and carry on in your psychical activity that reinforces the dominant neural net.

Rather than being overwhelmed by our reactions, awareness allows us to relax the grip of our current experience to notice how our mind gets stuck on one thing or another. Self-awareness and managing our emotions are processes based on a clear understanding of what's going on in ourselves. Understanding the extent of these perceptual biases, embedded in all human beings, will bring in moments of compassion for humanity.

Consider pausing and sensing how your perception of the world comes to you in your daily experience of life. Many triggers ignite in interpersonal relations. New mental models will support improved communication with others and therefore better self-other relationship skills. Instead of reacting to unconscious memory triggers, we start to understand where they are coming from and timestamp them as being part of the past and not happening currently.

Healing Toxic Shame

Shame can be another big hurdle to overcome. If your family members either explicitly or implicitly rejected you, you likely internalized the shame of being rejected. This flavor of emotional abuse is experienced as toxic shame. This means that you generally walk around feeling like there is something bad or wrong about you. Like a constant drone in the back of your mind, the DMN's negativity bias has taken root 24-7. You're stuck in negative rumination. Neural pathways have been laid down and it's going to require a special quality of attention to change the circuitry. First, you need to realize that your persistent negative experience of yourself and those around you has buried your natural gift of pure perception.

At some point either in early childhood or as a result of PTSD later on, you may have become 'hijacked' by the brain's anxiety programming. You are in limbic mode. Your red emotional brain is pinging wildly without the filter of your prefrontal cortex that can help you pause.

When you begin a healing process and wake up to this neural reaction-repetition, you start to see that all of your negative assessments and projections are coming out of the fear brain. You realize that the stressful environments that had previously triggered you can now come under your locus of control. You now look for healthy people with whom to experience secure attachment. Best of all, you finally learn to set boundaries with others where appropriate. You stop saying yes when your body says no. If you develop symptoms, you see it as a sign to regulate your emotions and sensory input.

Tips for Treating Depression, Anger and Negative Emotions

- Neuroplastic techniques like meditation, aromatherapy with citrus essential oils

- Exercise

- Anti-inflammatory diet

- Omega-3 EPA/DHA, B-complex

- Boost serotonin and/or dopamine with exercise and dietary supplements such as 5HTP, Serotone, Gabatone and Dopatone Active

- Emo-Sensory Therapy

Anxiety

When we are anxious, our working memory declines, which makes it very difficult to recall important information. Anxiety also decreases access to executive function in the prefrontal cortex and, therefore, makes it harder for us to complete tasks efficiently. When we feel anxious, poor self-regulation skills often kick into negative thought loops, which further decrease executive functioning. This in turns leads to inflexible thinking and, likely, poor social skills. This may result in the inability to be self- reflective and show empathy toward others.

Many people have predictable anxiety triggers like social demands and unexpected change, fear of new situations, fear of separation and emotionally stressful situations that occur daily. While anxious people have learned to medicate their anxiety with food and substances that work to calm them down, they need to learn ways to prevent anxiety triggers and build up social and emotional skills to cope with the moments when anxiety strikes in the first place.

Neurotransmitters and Anxiety

The neurobiology of anxiety can also be considered via brain chemistry and the activity of neurotransmitters. If you are an anxious person, the main neurotransmitters to consider are GABA and serotonin. Serotonin is found throughout the brain and the digestive system. While serotonin is known for mood, sleep and learning, GABA is the main inhibitory neurotransmitter needed to shift us out of anxiety and into relaxation.

If we can't balance the stress in our lives (perceived or real), we need to focus more on calming down the body and reducing sympathetic tone. GABA clicks us into parasympathetic mode - the only mode where healing can occur. Its main importance is that it's the only inhibitory neurotransmitter that can reach the brain stem and shut down the fight-flight-freeze reflex.

The Secret to Treating Anxiety

Those who have relentless anxiety may not have learned how to regulate the amygdala unless they've taken medications. They have never been taught the basics of brain structure and function and have yet to employ the underlying fixes that are needed to relieve them of their fiery emotional stress. Brain areas to consider for anxiety are the PFC, the amygdala, the hippocampus, the basal ganglia, the olfactory bulb and the right insular cortex.

- Meditation

- Emo-Sensory Therapy

- Essential oils

- Pranayama

- Relaxing music

- Exercise

- Omega-3 EPA/DHA, B-complex

- Dietary supplements such as GABA, Serotone, B6, magnesium and valerian found in Gabatone

Regulating the Subcortical Brain

For anxiety, we can regulate subcortical brain structures such as the amygdala (fear-emotion processing) with exercise, diaphragmatic breathing, essential oils, music and sound meditations. To decrease anxiety, you can also start anticipating upcoming or challenging emotional experiences and rehearsing responses and strategies. Start practicing relaxation techniques such as breathing, stretching and listening to calming music. Do emotional temperature taking by checking in with your body hourly and when you need to make decisions, ask, 'how do I feel right now?'

Here is a summary chart to simplify all the information that we have covered so far.

Personality Type	Traits	Disease Predisposition	Brain Structures	Brain Networks
TYPE A	Neuroticism Extraversion Aggression Motivation	Coronary Heart Disease Allergies Autoimmune Disease	Dorsolateral PFC Posterior Parietal Cortex	Central Executive Network (CEN) Default Mode Network (DMN) Hypothalamic-Pituitary-Adrenal-Axis (HPA)
TYPE C	Neuroticism Introversion Repressed Emotions Boundary Confusion	Cancer Infections Autoimmune Disease	Ventromedial Prefrontal Cortex Posterior Cingulate Cortex Anterior Cingulate Cortex Anterior Insular Cortex	Default Mode Network (DMN) Salience Network (SN) Hypothalamic-Pituitary-Adrenal-Axis (HPA)
TYPE D	Neuroticism Negative Affectivity Social Inhibition Harm Avoidance	Anxiety Depression Rumination Autoimmune Disease	Ventromedial Prefrontal Cortex Posterior Cingulate Cortex Amygdala Hippocampus Anterior Insular Cortex Anterior Cingulate Cortex	Default Mode Network (DMN) Salience Network (SN) Hypothalamic-Pituitary-Adrenal-Axis (HPA)
TYPE G	Introversion Neuroticism Rumination High Sensitivity Enhanced Cognitive Capacity	Anxiety Depression ADHD, OCD HSP, SPD Sensory Processing Sensitivity Environmental Sensitivity Allergies Autoimmune Disease	Basal Ganglia Motor Cortex Premotor Cortex Somatosensory Cortex Parietal Cortex Posterior Cingulate Cortex Thalamus Anterior Insular Cortex Anterior Cingulate Cortex Bilateral Temporal, Medial and Posterior Parietal Regions Occipitotemporal Regions Cerebellum	Central Executive Network (CEN) Default Mode Network (DMN) Salience Network (SN) Hypothalamic-Pituitary-Adrenal-Axis (HPA)

Looking through the Neurobiological Lens

Most of our understanding of autoimmune disease has come from cellular biology and consideration of the regulatory controls that keep the immune system balanced. Now, I want to take a step back and start considering autoimmune, sensory processing, learning, mental and emotional symptoms as stemming from brain circuits that give rise to trait expression.

When we look more deeply at the levers that control the immune system in the brain, we'll see that this is not just a cellular regulation issue, but also a self-regulation and emotional regulation issue. We can consider how to correct the unintegrated right brain, which may be deficient in terms of top-down PFC control over poor sensory processing and emotional regulation. When we understand the neural circuitry involved, we can better understand how this is stimulating our cellular responses and the manifestation of symptoms at the level of the physical body, the emotions and via our behaviors and personality tendencies.

After studying with Functional Neurologists who introduced me to the idea that sensory processing, affective and immune disorders, from anxiety to autism and autoimmunity, are due to a "right brain deficiency," I realized that very few people were teaching this valuable information. Since the right hemisphere has to do with regulating the immune system as well as emotional and sensory integration, it follows that supporting the right hemisphere to process sensory input as well as our emotions will in turn benefit the immune system.

The first thing to consider is that the immune system is a sensory processing system, which is governed by the hemispheres of the brain. The senses (like the immune system) are the first line of information processing that the nervous system uses to respond in an approach/avoid kind of way. The immune system can be seen as reflected in both the micro (cell danger response of cytokines and mitokines) and the macro in terms of behavioral responses.

If the sensory-motor system is shot, the immune system will act aberrantly. We used to think of immune dysfunction as stemming from genetic predisposition, e.g., inability to create regulatory balance, coming from deletion of hardwired genes that set us up for immune system failure in regulating threats. We now know that these threats extend to the emotional and sensory aspects of our being. From pathogenic to physical and emotional threats, the immune system is micro-processing every bit of information, good and bad.

As we gain insight into the functional connectivity required by the motor and sensory systems, and the inputs needed to improve connectivity in these brain regions, we can apply neuroscience to autoimmune disease, sensory processing, affective disorders and personality tendencies. The key is to start learning how to balance our brain hemispheres. That is, we get good at strengthening the connectivity of functionally disconnected areas that we can self-assess and implement in our own neuroplastic system.

We can globally start by supporting right and left hemisphere weaknesses, then target specific regions, e.g., the prefrontal cortex, amygdala, insular cortex, basal ganglia - sensory/visual/hearing areas of the brain that can be more functionally connected.

Neurobiological Deficits and Neurodegeneration

In recent years, developments in neuroscience have offered significant breakthroughs in understanding the inflammation, brain chemistry and neurobiology behind the behaviors associated with autoimmune, personality and neurodegenerative disorders.

In the functional neurology or hemispheric balance model, the left brain initiates immune system responses to infection, and the right side, when working normally, inhibits these responses from careening towards autoimmunity. If the right hemisphere is weak, autoimmunity, affective, learning and sensory issues may be a result. Adequate brain stimulation is important to make sure both hemispheres of our brain are balanced.

What if we thought about the things we diagnose as autoimmune disease, neuropsychiatric disorders and mood or personality trait expression as stemming from the same issue - a right hemisphere imbalance plus chronic inflammation? Instead of seeing all these things as disorders or diseases, we could look at them more as emotional/social, behavioral, learning and/or sensory challenges. At the end of the day, you will notice that they are all disorders of cognitive, motor and emotional regulation.

From this vantage point, you can evaluate what's preventing your immune system from learning and how to correct it. The solution is a comprehensive program that addresses all of these issues but is targeted toward the primary problem — what is termed a functional disconnection. Basically, a functional disconnection is a communication breakdown of neurons or groups of neurons in areas of the brain. Either there is a deficit in neuronal connectivity or neuronal firing starts getting asynchronous instead of firing together in a pattern called functional connectivity. When we can work at the level of cause of these brain-based imbalances we may see undesirable tendencies, patterns and behaviors resolve themselves.

Knowing your Neurobiological Deficits

Understanding yourself, your traits, gene markers and tendency to autoimmune disease expression has been the goal of both modern psychology and immunology. The field of Psycho-Neuro-Immunology (PNI) maps out the bidirectional relationship between our brain, emotions and the immune system. The Neuropsychology camp (application of neuroscience to psychology) goes even further in looking at the underlying neurobiological correlates of our emotional and psychological tendencies. A neurobiological correlate is the brain structure that lights up on fMRI tests, e.g., the amygdala in people with anxiety.

A better approach is to start looking at neurobiological deficits that exist prior to trait expression. This gives you the advantage of knowing the areas of disconnect and how to improve functional connectivity to decrease symptoms (trait or gene expression) and create neuroplasticity. This yields the most efficient solution to decreasing or getting rid of symptoms altogether.

Knowing your neurobiological deficits can give you even more information for not only prevention, but also for solution's sake. For example, knowing about the neurological correlates of anxiety, such as an increase of activity in the amygdala, can also lend insight into how to work with your predispositions.

Neurobiology and Neuropsychology

The same way as a gene marker such as HLA B27 may predispose you to an overactive immune response (phenotype expression); you can also look at your neurobiological deficit as the predisposing factor behind psychological and neuropsychiatric phenotype expression (from anxiety and depression to Alzheimer's).

The neuropsychological approach acknowledges that there is a neurological basis for what's going on behind the manifestation of psychological traits and even considers brain structures that are involved. For example, knowing that narcissists have a hard time being introspective because there may be decreased gray matter in the insula (which reveals a lack of functional connectivity in that area) could inform a Neuropsychologist's approach to treatment. From this perspective, you can see the root cause lies in decreased neural firing, which is a clue to target these parts of your brain to improve plasticity.

Neurobiological Substrates of Personality

From a neurobiological point of view traits such as negative affect and social inhibition may stem from a functionally disconnected brain, i.e., areas of the brain that are not connecting as well as they could be. Since negative affect has been identified as a psychological trait that leads to an increase in cytokine production, it's important to understand the status of brain circuits and neurobiological substrates (or brain structures) that give rise to this condition.

In a study of 263 people, negative affect related traits (neuroticism and harm avoidance) were associated with much more widely distributed reductions in white matter integrity (Xu et al., 2011). Individual differences in reactivity to negative emotional stimuli have also been shown, at the neural level, to be reflected in:

- Differences in gray matter volume or density in limbic regions
- Differences in the ventromedial prefrontal inhibition of brainstem nuclei involved in affective responses (Amat et al., 2008)
- Differences in the function of the corticotropin releasing hormone system that modulates the stress response (Ellis et al., 2006)
- Complex inhibitory and excitatory influences of different serotonin receptors in the ventromedial PFC, amygdala and other regions (Fisher et al., 2011)

- Structural or functional coupling between inferotemporal object recognition circuits and limbic affective circuits (Ahs et al., 2009)

Anxiety related traits such as neuroticism and harm avoidance are associated with gray matter volume reductions in memory and emotion linked medial temporal lobe (MTL) regions, such as the hippocampus and amygdala (Spampinato et al., 2009). Human studies have also found smaller MTL (medial temporal lobe) structures in patients with PTSD and other anxiety related disorders (Du et al., 2011).

What if we knew how to target the affected areas e.g. the amygdala, hippocampus and the medial temporal lobe? How would our health improve if we also supported neurotransmitters, cleaned up the environment of the brain and gut, practiced neuroplastic exercises, used music therapy, used specific essential oils and did an entire emo-sensory and immuno-makeover? How would that affect our personality development?

Functional Integration and Personality

The term neurobiology refers to both the nervous system and the immune system. If you look it up, you will also get the term functional integration. Functional integration refers to a smooth flow of information from the senses to the brain, which allows us to respond to stimuli in an evolutionarily efficient way. If there is any deficit of neural connections, this may result in symptoms of sensory deficit, neurological deficit and/or immune imbalance. The key to improving connectivity and immune balance is targeting the areas that need it most.

The immune system responds to all of the emotions and our senses, including touch, taste, smell, hearing and sight. We need to start regarding the immune system as an emo-sensory processing system that experiences a "systems error" in need of correction. Like a learning disorder, we can retrain the immune system to process/learn differently by hacking its master – the brain!

So, what comes first? Is it the neurobiological landscape (with its built-in deficits in certain regions of the brain, such as decreased grey matter in the right anterior insular cortex) that inhibits our ability to look within and introspect? Or is it the behavioral, emotional and sensory responses that shape the neurobiological landscape? We are finding out that we need to start with the neurobiological landscape and then look at stress, infection, trauma and chronic inflammation, which unfortunately can all happen simultaneously.

In the case of genetically primed autoimmune disease, sensory processing and affective issues, genes and traits may be set off because the right hemisphere is lacking accurate cognitive, sensory and emotional integration. However, with the correct neuroplastic training and emo-sensory inputs, we can regulate an immune system that's gone haywire.

Ultimately, it's about balancing both hemispheres of the brain through specific stimulation of deficient areas. We can start by determining overall brain health, assessing hemispheric dominance and seeing what brain regions need an extra boost in terms of plasticity in those areas.

Once we gain insight into the inputs needed to improve connectivity in brain regions, we can apply neuroscience to autoimmune disease, sensory processing, learning and affective disorders. The key is to start learning how to balance our brain hemispheres. That is, getting skilled at strengthening the connectivity of functionally disconnected areas that we can self-assess and implement in our own neuroplastic system.

We can globally start by supporting right and left hemisphere weaknesses, then target specific regions, e.g., the prefrontal cortex, amygdala, insular cortex and basal ganglia, along with sensory/visual/hearing (temporal-occipital-parietal) areas of the brain that can be more functionally connected. We can then apply remedies that drive neuroplasticity (i.e., functional connectivity in the middle-prefrontal cortex [social brain], limbic system [emotional brain] and PMRF [hindbrain or reptilian brain]).

We also need to clean up the environment of the brain and gut, give neurotransmitter support and build neuroplasticity with exercises and therapies, such as mindful and rhythmic movement, music, specific essential oils and a clean diet.

Psycho-Neuro-Immunology and Functional Neurology

The field of Psycho-Neuro-Immunology (PNI) characterizes the interface of the immune system with the brain and emotions. Evidence suggests that parts of the immune system may generate systemic responses in response to certain emotions. In a state of perpetual activation, immune mediators, such as cytokines, chemokines and free radicals, may cause tissue damage leading to chronic inflammation and subsequently increase the risk of neurobiological deficits and brain degeneration.

We need to start considering the truth about autoimmune disease patients. The truth is that while they do have trouble with sensory and emotional integration, we've been so focused on cellular biology that we have not yet considered the role of the right hemisphere in processing the senses and emotions and regulating immune function.

We have made a step toward this in our understanding of Psycho-Neuro-Immunology, in terms of emotional processing via the immune system, but we have not yet made the leap to nervous and immune integration (i.e., functional integration or neurobiological balance) that needs to occur.

Functional Neurology looks at the flow of information between the nervous system and immune system. Our nervous and immune systems are our primary motor and sensory processing systems. These are the main drivers of information from external environmental sources via the sensory system to the autonomic nervous system, the central nervous system (brain stem) and the limbic (emotional) system. The nervous and immune system both respond directly to internal thought cues and emotional stimuli, which then provoke responses in our physiology.

We now know that most animal species use the neuroendocrine stress axis (mainly the HPA) to integrate sensory input regarding habitat quality to inform the appropriate level of fear, withdrawal, avoidance, paranoia and other defensive behaviors (Diorio et al., 2000).

From the perspective of neuroscience, having unmet needs that we are unaware of is considered a brain disturbance that drives our thoughts, behavior and emotional reactions. For example, if our needs for safety aren't met, the brain goes into the fight/flight (sympathetic stress) mode of the nervous system. In this mode, stress hormones flood our system and we look only for ways to feel safe. If our reward seeking needs go unmet, we default into a state of frustration, clinging and grasping. And when our basic needs for connection go unmet, we can easily default into states of fear, paranoia, withdrawal and hopelessness.

However, when these needs are met, we feel safe, satisfied and connected and the parasympathetic system can take effect and keep us calm and at peace. It is only in this state that the body can repair itself and can achieve homeostasis or balance. The good news is that we can use techniques to evolve our brains and balance our nervous and immune system sooner rather than later. When we learn how to help the brain-immune system to learn, it changes the way we can take care of ourselves.

82

Emotional-Immune Connection

It has long been established in Traditional Chinese Medicine, and now more recently in Psycho-Neuro-Immunology (PNI), that emotional dynamics can either perpetuate or ameliorate our physical health problems. We now know that not only is there a bidirectional communication system between the immune system and the brain, there is also bidirectional communication between the brain and the endocrine system, and the brain and the gut. The messenger molecules that link these systems are called neuropeptides. Dr. Candace Pert was the first to call these messenger molecules the "molecules of emotion." Neuropeptides are now considered the material equivalent of thoughts. Whenever we think, imagine, laugh or have an emotional reaction, we make neuropeptides that bind to and communicate with our immune cells.

Dr. Pert also found that opiate receptors, densely concentrated in the limbic brain (especially the hippocampus and the amygdala), occur in every other part of the body. The implication is that emotions are not generated by the brain but by the cells themselves. Since these receptor-bearing cells reside all over our bodies, all emotional experience also occurs in the blood, organs, muscles, tissue and bones at the same time as they are registered in the brain. So, the immune cells are literally listening to the conversations you are having with yourself when you are thinking or meditating. Moving on from Psycho-Neuro-Immunology (PNI), we will now enter discussion of autoimmune personality needs and inclusion of the role of the brain, as well as the effect of brain imbalances on personality.

The Right Brain and Personality Traits

When Functional Neurologists refer to right hemispheric weakness, they mean that the orbital frontal cortex and the hyperdirect pathway (in the basal ganglia) are both immature. This initially makes sense when you start to consider how people who have developmental issues (such as ADHD) demonstrate a lack of control of the orbital frontal cortex and the hyperdirect pathway, due to the fact that these structures are immature. This would lead to hyperkinetic movement.

Notably, in neurodegenerative disorders, mental health issues and autoimmune disease, the root cause is also explained by the same fact that there is no regulatory control at the same locations. That is, the hyperdirect pathway and the orbitofrontal cortex (OFC) are under-functioning while the left dorsolateral prefrontal cortex and posterior parietal cortex are firing heavily. This reflects as left brain dominance with a weak right hemisphere. In these cases, there will likely be hyperkinetic movement and behavior (ADHD, OCD), hyperkinetic thought (repetitive thoughts, rumination) and/or "hyperkinetic" immune cell responses, i.e., autoimmune reactions.

In the functional neurology or hemispheric balance model, the left-brain initiates immune system responses to infection and the right side, when working normally, inhibits these responses from careening towards autoimmunity. If the right hemisphere is immature or weak, autoimmunity, affective, learning, behavioral and sensory processing issues may be a result. Therefore, precise brain stimulation is important to make sure both hemispheres are balanced.

Personality traits can help you learn about functional connectivity in your brain. Think of the brain as being at a loss in terms of having a profound lack of sensory, cognitive and emotional stimulation, processing and integration. This would lead to heightened sensitivity and emotional issues, ranging from anxiety to depression to social inhibition, harm avoidance and negative affect. These deficiencies are all considered right brain deficits in specific processing centers.

When we view emotional and sensory deficits as a right brain deficiency, we can identify brain areas, e.g., the temporal, occipital and parietal lobes, the somatosensory and motor cortices, the right insular cortex (for sensing oneself internally), the basal ganglia (for sensing your body in relation to the environment) and/or the cerebellum, which has to do with timing and rhythm.

In terms of personality traits, the left brain is associated with approach behavior (extraversion, reward seeking), while the right brain is about avoidance (introversion and harm avoidance). This is reflected both in our immune system (the left brain senses and turns on a response, the right brain puts the brakes on the attack of foreign proteins) and in our behavior.

The right hemisphere of the brain regulates impulsivity, attention and socially appropriate behavior. With decreased right brain activity, a person may be hyperactive, oppositional, disruptive and even aggressive. The remedy is to improve vertical integration of body sensations and emotions on the right side, along with supporting the flow of information from the right hemisphere to the left (aka horizontal integration). This will lead to hemispheric balance. We can look at our symptoms as stemming from a right brain deficiency. We can also make sense of our unconscious drives stemming from hard wired neural grooves that the conscious mind has yet to encounter. This not only helps us tease apart and understand our basic drives, but is also an entry point to wholeness and integration of ego and the self.

So, we keep on going back to the brain-based understanding of immune dysfunction, autoimmune reactions and trait expression as triggered by emotional regulation and sensory processing issues. If these issues surface in our lives, we can see them as an adaptive challenge and instead of being upset about the deficits, we can focus on improving functional connectivity. The answer is simple – we can use neuroplastic and sensory stimulation to create immune balance.

Investigating the neurobiological mechanisms underlying personality will continue to advance our understanding of individual differences in brain structure and function, ultimately revealing differences in behavior. For now, we can focus on developing models to rehabilitate neurobiological deficits and repair functional connectivity through neuroplastic exercises.

Upping Your Adaptive Strategy

While most practitioners are now familiar with the merit of studying and considering PNI in our recommendations for clients, e.g., encouraging positive emotions and mindsets, this ultimately fails since most of us have never addressed the brain areas that are in need of support. This requires taking a look at the dominant neural nets that may be impeding your agency in feeling better.

In this book, we have explored autoimmune personality trait expression as stemming from a combination of highly charged cognitive, emotional and sensory neural circuitry that drives the expression of traits that, in turn, further drive autoimmune reactions. Indeed a hyper-brain can cause a hyper-body and here we will start to understand autoimmune disease through a new neurobiological lens. Improved knowledge of our personality tendencies and brain type can help us journey through disease to wellness. Besides some of the strategies we have already considered, those with autoimmune disease also need to know about improving functionality of the sensory/motor system with appropriate stimulation.

Epigenetics, Neuroplasticity and Immunoplasticity

Extensive research and in-depth study of epigenetics has shown that the brain is not static but remarkably adaptable and able to create new neural pathways in response to stimuli in the environment. This branch of science is called neuroplasticity. If you consider that from a neurobiological perspective, the immune system is a circulating nervous system, therefore, neuroplasticity = immunoplasticity. The suggestion is that doing anything that encourages neuroplasticity will also create immunoplasticity. The result will be a more balanced immune system.

From a neurobiological level, we can see that the functional controls of the right brain are failing. We can support the immune system on a cellular level by starting with a clean diet. The next step is to access the right brain via cortical stimulation as well as subcortical stimulation (i.e., the limbic and hindbrain). This is the missing link in addressing immune imbalances at the level of sensory and emotional experiences.

We can start with the application of neuro-immuno-relaxation techniques and Emo-Sensory Therapy to relax the limbic system and calm the sympathetic nervous system, allowing the brain to heal. In this way, the brain and immune system can learn more efficiently. Only then will the immune system be primed to accurately integrate our sensory and emotional experiences. At first, we intentionally apply neuroplastic practices nonstop over six weeks to develop plasticity. Then, we take a break and move forward using them as needed - for example, after a stressful experience where you feel your body still is holding unprocessed sensory and emotional experiences.

Then, we can simultaneously apply brain based exercises, e.g., yoga, Tai Chi, Qi Gong, Brain Balance, swimming and any other mindful exercises to consciously integrate sensory/motor experience into physical activity. We can also use high intensity interval training (HIIT) exercises to engage the basal ganglia (which has to do with movement and motivation) and power up the cerebellum to improve brain rhythm and timing. Regular exercise is fine, too, but you are going to get more of an impact if you can combine awareness with exercise. We can add to that introspection technologies, such as meditation and viscerosomatic body sensing, in order to build up plasticity in the prefrontal and right insular cortices. All of this will go a long way to balance a right hemisphere deficiency and decrease everything from autoimmune reactions to anxiety, depression, and rumination.

A brain-based understanding of immune dysfunction sees that emotional and sensory processing deficits are just waiting for a neuroplastic challenge in order to yield a more balanced immune system. Based on my research into how to access the immune system via the sensory/emotional and motor systems, I suggest a novel 7-step method for immune balance.

THE ULTIMATE
MIND-BRAIN-BODY APPROACH TO HEALING
AUTOIMMUNE DISEASE

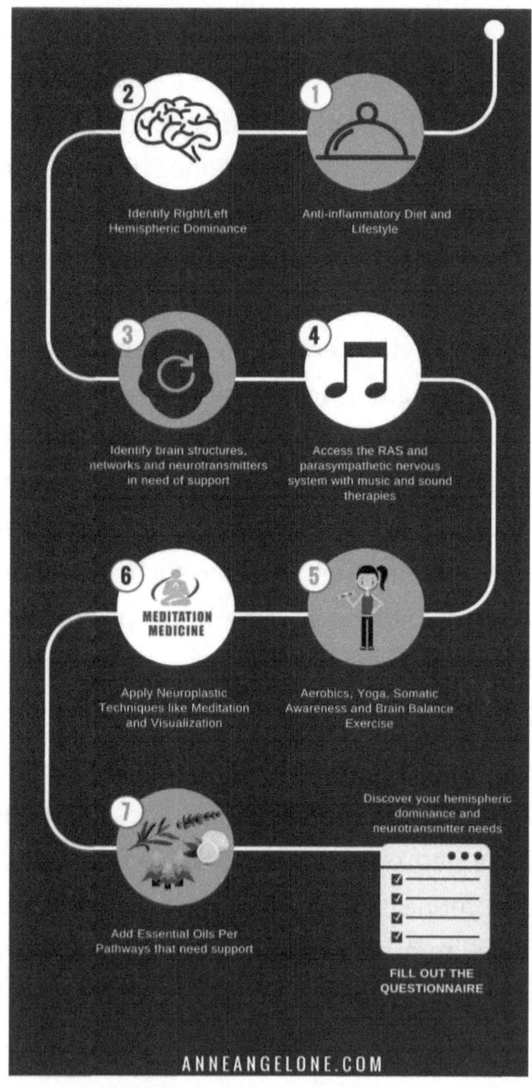

7 Steps to Immune Balance

1. Start with an anti-inflammatory diet and lifestyle

2. Determine hemispheric dominance

3. Identify brain structures, networks and neurotransmitters in need of support

4. Access the parasympathetic nervous system with music and sound meditations

5. Include specific exercises like yoga

6. Apply neuroplastic techniques like meditation

7. Add essential oils per pathways that need support

And so, with a new understanding of neurobiological flow, not only can we support the cortical brain, but also the subcortical brain, to regulate the emotional-sensory system and, therefore, the immune system.

Supporting the Brain and the Immune System

To support the immune system, we need to first start thinking more about stabilizing neural connections that are showing signs of degeneration or loss of function. In this model, when the immune system is out of balance, we need to backtrack and identify what parts of the brain are deficient and leading to the downstream effects of imbalance. Digest that for a moment. This is the connection that will lead to the next phase of consideration for autoimmune disease, which will now require you, the reader, to make a leap in understanding – the leap from cellular biology to neurobiology.

Once we identify the deficient areas, the remedies are exercise, good diet and sensory regulation, which includes essential oil stimulation and music therapy based on the part of the brain that needs it most. For example, a person who is highly anxious with a fiery amygdala would do well with calming instrumental music or nature sounds to relax. You can also use other sensory techniques to enhance the specific outcome you'd like. For example, you can add essential oils for calming the mind (lavender and bergamot) while you're practicing yoga. This sets the stage for a pleasant multi-sensory experience.

Preparing the Brain to Learn

Many doctors and health care professionals are not comfortable with or trained in neuroscience, so it helps to learn the key principles on your own to facilitate the nervous and immune systems' ability to process information. In teaching the nervous-immune system to learn, you can identify what you need to listen to, see and feel in the most precise, sensate way that makes you feel safe, satisfied and included in humanity.

When you are first learning how to stimulate and rewire your brain, i.e., your nervous-immune system, you begin by first figuring out what your sensory-body and emotional needs are. Once you know what you need, you can practice until it becomes automatic.

Music, sound and light are powerful teaching tools to use when you are trying to encourage your brain and immune system to learn something new. The best way to prepare the brain to learn is to connect it with something it already likes, e.g., music, nature sounds and colors. One secret healing tool is to develop your own music, sounds and visualizations as an emo-sensory learning strategy. You can also check out my Emo-Sensory Therapy 10 Week Program mp3's here.

Consistently applying neuroplastic strategies will yield a more balanced immune system. To master the brain-immune system, you'll need to not only power up the cortex with exercise, but support the parasympathetic nervous system (at the subcortical level) to yield nervous, emotional and sensory regulation. This can be accomplished with, yoga, breathing, essential oils, therapeutic music and sound meditations.

At first, the approach includes intentionally applying neuroplastic practices nonstop over six weeks to develop plasticity. Then you take a break, followed by using them on an as needed basis. I have created an Autoimmune Brain Balance program in my studio for this express purpose; they are available for review on my website.

And so, with a new understanding of neurobiological flow, not only can we support the cortical brain but also the sub cortical brain to regulate the emotional-sensory system, i.e., the immune system.

Exercise

It is well known that movement powers the prefrontal cortex, but many people who lead intellectually challenging lives tend not to get enough exercise and need to move their bodies.

Exercise can impact the prefrontal cortex, motor cortex, cerebellum, proprioception and sensory perception. By creating a smooth flow of sensory and motor processing, you are a retraining the nervous and immune systems. This is the secret behind techniques such as Feldenkrais, yoga and other mindfulness-movement techniques, including mindful walking, Qi Gong and Tai Chi. Essentially, you are doing neuroplastic techniques that are training the smooth flow of muscle coordination with simultaneous mindful awareness of the sensations you are feeling. Sensory/motor exercises encourage an awareness of your body/limbs in space to increase proprioception, while being mindful of yourself breathing increases interoception. If you're disciplined about implementing change, you will likely notice results (that is, better global connectivity) over six weeks' time.

Increasing Vagal Tone

The vagus nerve (cranial nerve X) is constantly sending information from your viscera to your brain. It controls heart rate, gastrointestinal motility, enzyme and HCl secretion, hormone secretion and gluconeogenesis.

A lesser known fact is that the vagus nerve is involved in the inflammatory reflex that controls innate immune responses and inflammation during pathogen invasion and tissue injury. Once innate immune responses are activated by pathogens, molecular patterns are recognized by sensors on the immune cell surfaces, e.g., Toll-like receptors (TLRs) signal increased production and release of tumor necrosis factor (TNF), IL-6 and other proinflammatory cytokines.

When innate immune regulation fails, pro-inflammatory cytokine activity and chronic inflammation result. This chronic inflammatory state underlies a range of disease syndromes, including sepsis, rheumatoid arthritis, inflammatory bowel disease and other inflammatory and autoimmune disorders.

Brain-immune communication is the key to controlling inflammation. When afferent vagus nerve fibers sense peripheral inflammatory molecules (cytokines), they convey signals to the brainstem nuclei, the hypothalamus and forebrain regions associated with integration of visceral sensory information, as well as coordination of autonomic function and behavioral responses (Pavlov et al., 2003). Throughout this process the efferent vagus nerves regulate proinflammatory cytokine production and inflammation. This mechanism is referred to as the inflammatory reflex.

Efferent vagus nerve cholinergic signaling in brain-to-immune communication has been shown to suppress proinflammatory cytokine levels. The fact that acetylcholine itself has been shown to inhibit the release of inflammatory cytokines TNF, IL-1β and IL-18 led to the definition of the cholinergic anti-inflammatory pathway as the efferent vagus nerve-based arm of the inflammatory reflex (Pavlov et al., 2012).

Efferent vagus nerve endings might directly regulate the immune function by releasing acetylcholine, which has been implicated in the suppression of inflammation in experimental settings of hemorrhagic shock, ileus, inflammatory bowel disease, autoimmune myocarditis and other inflammatory and autoimmune conditions. Importantly, many of these disorders are associated with decreased vagal tone, so enhancement of vagus tone could yield a therapeutic effect for the above conditions (ibid, 2012).

In modern times, we are perhaps too inclined to retain sympathetic tone and thus need many classes on stress reduction, meditation and yoga to learn how to intentionally shift the balance. This may be especially useful to the vulnerable brains out there who suffer with extra inflammation from autoimmune disease. We also know that stress causes sympathetic dominance and is in part due to under-activity or deficient amounts of the inhibitory neurotransmitter GABA.

Since low GABA activity occurs in anxiety disorders, post-traumatic stress disorder, depression and chronic pain, it's important to work on toning the parasympathetic nervous system to make sure that everyday stressors don't get the best of us and knock us off guard. Practices such as sound meditation, singing, chanting, yoga postures and breathing techniques are excellent for increasing vagal tone.

Neuroplastic Strategies

You likely have now come to the realization that neuroplastic techniques are literally right in front of our senses. The easiest way to access the limbic structures is through the senses. When we alter our sensory experiences, immune system imbalances (when thought of as a sensory and emotional processing error) can be healed via new information being fed to the senses and the emotions. Knowing the brain structures that are in need of support, you can immediately apply action steps to flood the system with as much precise emotional, physical and sensory support that you need. We can then consider strategies that drive neuroplasticity in the prefrontal cortex (social brain), limbic system (emotional brain) and the pontomedullary reticular formation (hindbrain). Neuroplastic strategies include:

- Exercise
- Meditation
- Essential oils
- Music
- Sound Meditation
- Diet
- Yoga
- Supplements
- Acupuncture

You can also use other sensory techniques along with these to bolster the specific outcome you'd like. For example, you can diffuse essential oils for attention and memory (pine, eucalyptus, sage) while you're using other techniques, thereby increasing a multi-sensory experience for the parts of the brain that need it most. If you are disciplined in your approach, you are likely to see better functional connectivity within six weeks. The trick is figuring out the best strategies that work for you.

Gravity

What is your relationship with gravity? Our sense of ourselves in space can vary throughout our lifetimes, especially those of us who have lost mobility as a result of tissue destruction. As you now know, the inflammatory reflex, refers to the mechanism of controlling inflammation in the brain and body. Since this reflex can be altered by gravity, those with autoimmune disease (who experience recurrent and remittent flaring and resultant brain-body inflammation) might want to consider their relationship to gravity.

Part of the reason why yoga is so beneficial is that it takes into account our relationship to gravity with inversion poses, balance postures and use of sandbags and bolsters. Since proprioception (our sense of ourselves in space) affects the immune system, it makes sense to improve this ability with specific exercises like yoga and other brain balancing activities.

Supporting Your Mitochondria

At the end of the day, getting the cells out of the danger response and back to homeostasis is the goal of therapy. This is yet another reason to take relaxation and meditation seriously. Also, Traditional Chinese Medicine has been using adaptogenic herbs for centuries to help us to adapt to stressors in the environment. In fact one of the most studied adaptogens used to protect mitochondria and support mitochondrial metabolism is panax ginseng (Li et al, 2009). Besides reducing stress, you can also protect your mitochondria from damage and speed repair with the following supplements:

- Magnesium
- NAC (N-Acetyl Cysteine)
- Co-Q 10
- Alpha Lipoic Acid
- Acetyl-L-Carnitine

Intentional Self-Emotional-Regulation Diary

Being intentional is a higher brain function, which we initially may need to train, especially if it's not automatically helping you course correct and you keep running into the same old thoughts, behaviors and problems. Taking into account how our bodies experience space/time through gravity and circadian rhythms, we can support sleep cycles to match the rhythm of the day and seasons.

Since at first we may do well with some discipline, here is a starting dialogue to have with yourself. Feel free to use this as a template and add your own questions and script. The fact that it's an exercise in self-emotional-regulation is what counts.

Record Observable Facts:

Morning

- What time did you go to bed?
- What time did you awaken?
- How many hours did you sleep?
- What was your mood upon awakening? Why?
- What self or emotional regulation exercises did you use to start your day?
- How long was your morning practice?

Review your day

- How well did you self-regulate today?
- How well did you emotionally-regulate today?
- How many hours did you spend in useless company or on useless activities?

- How did you keep your energy intact?
- Did you eat properly?
- What did you eat, and how did it affect your consciousness, mind, emotions and body?
- Did you eat consciously?
- What was your mood today? Why?
- What effect did this have on yourself and others?
- What practices did you use today? How much?
- What physical exercise did you get today?
- How did it affect your consciousness, emotions and body?
- Did you restrain your emotional impulses today? Which ones were visible to you today?
- How many times did your negative emotions appear? For how long? How did you handle that?
- How many times did your alienation-dissociation or disconnection appear?
- For how long? How did you handle that?
- How many lies did you believe and tell yourself today? How did you make up for that?
- Did you fail to control a harmful habit? Which, and how are you dealing with yourself?

Before bed

- Rate the quality of your concentration today: 0 is worst, 10 is best. Explain why your concentration is at this level.
- How much did you meditate today?
- Did you do an intentional practice of interoception? Did you try to connect brain, breath and body? How long did you practice?

- Can you sense any neuroplastic changes occurring that reflect in better self and emotional regulation skills?
- What virtue did you work on developing? What did you learn about it?
- What harmful qualities are you trying to correct? What did you learn about it?
- What is the chief obstacle impeding your healing? What is the antidote to that obstacle? Did you apply the antidote today?

Summary

Rate your day:

Based on everything above, summarize where you invested the most effort and energy today:

- I invested most of my energy in self-healing.
- I invested most of my energy into external circumstances (work, home, school, family).
- I invested most of my energy into emotional habits.
- I invested most of my energy into intellectual habits.
- I invested most of my energy into physical habits or worldly activities.
- What will you improve tomorrow?

Final Thoughts

Our society demands extraversion and strong left brain function. We are all trained to be extraverts for the sake of surviving in the world even though it may not feel natural to us. Personality traits may be the first place to start when we want to understand our cognitive, emotional and behavioral tendencies. Personality traits may tip you off to the possibility that you could have issues e.g. with e.g. high sensitivity, rumination, depression, anxiety and autoimmune reactions. In this way, personality traits may be looked at as risk factors for dis-ease. Being familiar with your personality traits is similar to knowing what genes might predispose you to your particular autoimmune disease. While genes and traits may predispose you to disease, you can rig your environment to remove triggers that set off gene and trait expression in the first place. We can also work on improving global connectivity in the brain to add to this effect.

The Autoimmune Brain, Mood and Personality Questionnaire

Today, maybe more than ever, we need to support our brain and nervous/immune systems to deal with the many toxic insults we encounter. This Autoimmune Brain, Mood and Personality questionnaire is a brain-based mood and personality profile. In this questionnaire you will find questions relating to general brain health, sensitivity, anxiety, depression, anger, inflammation, emotional and sensory intelligence (i.e., how well you can regulate your emotions and integrate sensory data).

Remember that, as in any system, it is sometimes difficult to classify a person as a single type. There are many different moods, attitudes, behaviors and actions considered that may not all fit into one category, and you may find yourself noticing you have more Yes or No answers in a particular section. Use this new data to inform brain health, hemispheric balance and increased awareness of your dominant functions. You can use this information to get a snapshot of general brain health and right-left brain dominance as well as tendencies to rumination, depression and heightened sensitivity that impact the Autoimmune Personality.

Neurobiology meets Neuropsychology
and Personality Neuroscience
The
AUTOIMMUNE
Personality
QUESTIONNAIRE

SECTION 1 General Screening

	YES	NO
Diagnosed with an autoimmune disease	☐	☐
Emotionally depressed	☐	☐
Emotionally compulsive	☐	☐
Emotionally anxious	☐	☐
Eczema	☐	☐
Suffers from Irritable Bowel Syndrome	☐	☐
Chronic fatigue syndrome	☐	☐
Food sensitivities	☐	☐
Environmental sensitivities	☐	☐
Fibromyalgia	☐	☐
Allergies	☐	☐
Asthma	☐	☐
Sensory processing sensitivities	☐	☐
Low muscle tone	☐	☐
Fidgety- sensation seeker	☐	☐
Poor sense of body in space	☐	☐

SECTION 2 Brain Health	**YES**	**NO**
Inability to concentrate	☐	☐
Difficulty planning or problem solving	☐	☐
Cold hands and feet	☐	☐
Experiences frequent memory lapses	☐	☐
A loss of smell to foods	☐	☐
Difficulty sleeping	☐	☐
Has episodes of dizziness or light-headedness	☐	☐
Brain fog (unclear thoughts or concentration)	☐	☐
Constipation or irregular bowel movements	☐	☐
Difficulty swallowing supplements	☐	☐
Experiences difficulty with balance	☐	☐
Difficulty with right/left discrimination	☐	☐
Sloppy handwriting	☐	☐
Reduced function in overall hearing	☐	☐
Difficulty recognizing symbols, words, letters	☐	☐

SECTION 3 TYPE A Personality

	YES	NO
Aggressive	☐	☐
Motivated	☐	☐
Extraverted	☐	☐
Obsessive	☐	☐
Blunt and/or rude	☐	☐
Impatient	☐	☐
Driven	☐	☐
Ambitious	☐	☐
Competitive	☐	☐
Perfectionist	☐	☐
Workaholic	☐	☐
Easily angered	☐	☐
Stressed and anxious	☐	☐
Unhealthy dependence on external rewards such as wealth, status or power	☐	☐

SECTION 4 TYPE C Personality	YES	NO
Emotionally repressed	☐	☐
Ignores or suppresses significant feelings	☐	☐
Unable to express anger	☐	☐
Inability to recognize your own needs	☐	☐
Constantly doing things for others	☐	☐
No time for yourself	☐	☐
Calm, outwardly rational and unemotional demeanor	☐	☐
Agreeable	☐	☐
Tendency to conform to the wishes of others	☐	☐
Lack of assertiveness	☐	☐
Inclination toward feelings of helplessness or hopelessness	☐	☐
Inability to defend personal integrity	☐	☐
Tends to be codependent and has trouble saying "no"	☐	☐
Has a distorted and unstable self-image or sense of self	☐	☐
Introverted – recharges with alone time	☐	☐
Passive – to avoid conflict	☐	☐
Excessive kindness	☐	☐
Unobtrusiveness	☐	☐
Self depreciation	☐	☐
Perfectionist	☐	☐

SECTION 5 TYPE D Personality

	YES	NO
Negative view about self	☐	☐
Shyness, fear in groups	☐	☐
Fear of embarrassment	☐	☐
Fear of failure, perfectionism	☐	☐
Feel like you don't fit in	☐	☐
Difficulty understanding social situations	☐	☐
Has feelings of isolation	☐	☐
Difficulty understanding others' thoughts and feelings	☐	☐
Feels as if missing the conversation gene	☐	☐
Poor eye contact	☐	☐
Inhibits emotions in social interactions	☐	☐
Difficulty making friendships	☐	☐
Avoids expressing negative emotions in social situations	☐	☐
Fear of social disapproval	☐	☐
On constant lookout for danger – vigilant	☐	☐
Underlying anxiety or negativity	☐	☐
Insecure, low self-esteem	☐	☐
Depressed	☐	☐
Constant feelings of overwhelm	☐	☐
Angry	☐	☐

Irritable ☐ ☐

Prone to fear, disgust, anxiety and worry ☐ ☐

Harm avoidant – prefers activities that are safe ☐ ☐

History of traumatic event in early childhood ☐ ☐

Feelings of a "knot" in your stomach ☐ ☐

Startles easily ☐ ☐

Dysphoric mood ☐ ☐

SECTION 6 TYPE G Personality	YES	NO
Very curious and freely approaches new situations	☐	☐
Highly verbal	☐	☐
Analytical thinker	☐	☐
Good at memorizing large amounts of data	☐	☐
Avid reader	☐	☐
Searches for truth, justice and understanding	☐	☐
Conscientious	☐	☐
Love of problem solving	☐	☐
Motivated by ideas	☐	☐
Fidgety, can't sit still	☐	☐
Inability to handle stress – easily overwhelmed	☐	☐
Identifies with the feelings of others	☐	☐
Empathic	☐	☐
Anxiety	☐	☐
Depression	☐	☐
Painfully sensitive to criticism	☐	☐
Physical response to emotions (stomach aches, headaches)	☐	☐
Easily bothered by noise, lights and smells	☐	☐

Very perceptive and insightful	☐	☐
Struggles with mood swings	☐	☐
Requires a large amount of downtime	☐	☐
Highly intuitive to others' feelings	☐	☐
Thin skinned or feels emotionally porous	☐	☐
Startles easily	☐	☐
Sensitive to perfumes, foods, alcohol, etc.	☐	☐
Avoids negative and/or violent movies	☐	☐
Experiences sensory overload	☐	☐
Easily overwhelmed at parties or in large crowds	☐	☐
Perfectionist	☐	☐

SECTION 7 SEROTONIN	YES	NO
Loss of pleasure in hobbies and interests	☐	☐
Has had bouts of depression	☐	☐
Struggles with feelings of sadness	☐	☐
Worries	☐	☐
Inability to fall into deep, restful sleep	☐	☐
Noticeable loss of enjoyment in life	☐	☐
Feelings of sadness in winter or in overcast weather	☐	☐
Loss of enthusiasm for favorite activities	☐	☐
Loss of enjoyment in friendships and relationships	☐	☐
Susceptible to pain – low pain threshold	☐	☐

SECTION 8 DOPAMINE

	YES	NO
Lacks feelings of contentment	☐	☐
Desires to isolate from others	☐	☐
Chronic feelings of emptiness	☐	☐
Feelings of worthlessness	☐	☐
Feelings of hopelessness	☐	☐
Disinterest in hobbies, social activities or work	☐	☐
Anger and aggression when stressed	☐	☐
Unexplained lack of concern for family and friends	☐	☐
Inability to finish tasks	☐	☐
Impatient and easily frustrated	☐	☐

SECTION 9 GABA

	YES	NO
Feelings of nervousness or panic for no reason	☐	☐
Feelings of dread	☐	☐
Feelings of being overwhelmed for no reason	☐	☐
Feelings of guilt about everyday decisions	☐	☐
Restless mind	☐	☐
Inability to turn off the mind when relaxing	☐	☐
Feelings of inner tension	☐	☐
Low level anxiety	☐	☐
Seeks safety and security	☐	☐

SECTION 10 ACETYLCHOLINE

	YES	NO
Decrease in visual imagery (shapes and images)	☐	☐
Difficulty calculating numbers	☐	☐
Difficulty recognizing names and faces	☐	☐
Decrease in comprehension	☐	☐
Decrease in creativity	☐	☐
Occurrence of memory lapses	☐	☐
Disorganized attention	☐	☐
Difficulty finding words when speaking	☐	☐
Difficulty spelling familiar words	☐	☐
Difficulty with directions/maps	☐	☐

References

Ahs, F. et al., (2009). Disentangling the web of fear: amygdala reactivity and functional connectivity in spider and snake phobia. *Psychiatry Research, 172*(2), 103–108.

Amat, J. et al., (2008). Activation of the ventral medial prefrontal cortex during an uncontrollable stressor reproduces both the immediate and long term protective effects of behavioral control. *Neuroscience, 154*(4), 1178–1186.

Anticevic, A. et al., The role of default network deactivation in cognition and disease. Trends in Cognitive Sciences, 16 (2012), pp. 584-592.

Aron, E. et al., Adult Shyness: The Interaction of Temperamental Sensitivity and an Adverse Childhood Environment. Sage Journals. February 1, 2005

Bagnato, G. et al., Comparison of levels of anxiety and depression in patients with autoimmune and chronic-degenerative rheumatic: preliminary data. Reumatismo. 2006 Jul-Sep;58(3):206-11.

Baker, GH (1982): Life events before the onset of rheumatoid arthritis. *Psychotherapy and Psychosomatics,* 38(1): 173-7.

Bergnik, V. et al., (2014): Autoimmunity, inflammation and psychosis: a search for peripheral markers. *Biological Psychiatry, 75,* 324–331.

Chen, S. J. et al., (2012). Prevalence of autoimmune diseases in in-patients with schizophrenia: nationwide population-based study. British Journal of Psychiatry, 200, 374–380.

Cohen, M. et al., Connectivity-based segregation of the human striatum predicts personality characteristics. Nat. Neuroscience., 12 (2009), pp. 32-34

Damoiseaux, et al. Consistent resting-state networks across healthy subjects. PNAS September 12, 2006.

Cullen, A. E. et al., Associations between non-neurological autoimmune disorders and psychosis: A Meta-Analysis. *Biological Psychiatry.* June 2018.

Diana, R. et al., (1985): Personality aspects in multiple sclerosis. *Italian Journal of Neurological Science*, 6(4): 415-23.

Dickerson, Sally. et al., Immunological Effects of Induced Shame and Guilt. Psychosomatic Medicine. January 2004.

Diorio, J. et al., A DNA array study of hippocampal gene expression regulated by maternal behavior in infancy. *Soc. Neuroscience. Abstracts*, 26 (2000), p. 1366.

Du, M. et al. (2011). Voxelwise meta analysis of gray matter reduction in major depressive disorder. *Progress in Neuropsychopharmacology Biological Psychiatry, 36*(1), 11–16.

Eaton, W. et al., (2006). Association of schizophrenia and autoimmune diseases: linkage of Danish national registers. *American Journal of Psychiatry, 163,* 521–528.

Ehlers, U. Enduring psychobiological effects of childhood adversity. Psychoneuroendocrinology (2013). 2013 Sep; 38(9):1850-7.

Ellis, B. et al., (2006). The stress response systems: Universality and adaptive individual differences. *Developmental Review, 26*(2), 175–212.

Fisher, P. et al., (2011). Medial prefrontal cortex serotonin 1A and 2A receptor binding interacts to predict threat related amygdala reactivity. *Biology of Mood Anxiety Disorders*, *1*(1), 2.

Frank, E. et al., 2006. Genetic predisposition to anxiety-related behavior determines coping style, neuroendocrine responses, and neuronal activation during social defeat. *Behav. Neurosci.* 120:60–71.

Gong, Y. Chronic mild stress damages mitochondrial ultrastructure and function in mouse brain. Neuroscience Letters. Volume 488, Issue 1, 13 January 2011, Pages 76-80.

Karpinski, R. et al., High intelligence: A risk factor for psychological and physiological overexcitabilities. *Science Direct*. September 2017.

Klaassen, K. et al., Distressed personality is associated with lower psychological well-being and life satisfaction. Clinical Rheumatology. 2012 Apr; 31(4):661-7.

Li XT. et al., Regulation on energy metabolism and protection on mitochondria of Panax ginseng polysaccharide. Am J Chin Med. 2009; 37(6):1139-52.

Mate, Gabor. When The Body Says No. John Wiley and Sons, 2003.

Marzieh, S. et al., Personality dimensions and type D personality in female patients with ulcerative colitis. J Res Med Sci. 2012 Oct; 17(10): 898–904.

Medford, N., et al Conjoint activity of anterior insular and anterior cingulate cortex: awareness and response. Brain Structure and Function, 214 (2010), pp. 535-549.

McEwen, B. S. (1999). 'Lifelong effects of hormones on brain development: Relationship to health and disease'. In Extreme Fear, Shyness, and Social Phobia: Origins, Biological Mechanisms, and Clinical Outcomes, eds. L. Schmidt & J. Schulkin. New York: Oxford University Press.

Naviaux, R.K. Metabolic features of the cell danger response. *Mitochondrion* 16, 7-17 (2014).

Otto, R. et al., Psycho-social and emotional disturbance in systemic lupus erythematosus. Med J Aust. 1967 Sep 9; 2(11):488-93.

Pavlov, VA. et al., The cholinergic anti-inflammatory pathway: a missing link in neuroimmunomodulation. Molecular Medicine. 2003 May-Aug; 9(5-8):125-34.

Pavlov, V. et al., The vagus nerve and the inflammatory reflex—linking immunity and metabolism. Nat Rev Endocrinol. 2012 Dec; 8(12): 743–754.

Picard, M. et al., A Mitochondrial Health Index Sensitive to Mood and Caregiving Stress. Biological Psychiatry. Volume 84, Issue 1, 1 July 2018, Pages 9-17.

Sakami, S. et al., November 2004. Positive coping up- and down-regulates *in vitro* cytokine productions from T-cells dependent on stress levels. *Psychother. Psychosom.* 73:243–251.

Seden, D. et al., The Effect of Type D Personality on Quality of Life in Patients with Multiple Sclerosis. Noro Psikiyatr Ars. 2017 Sep; 54(3): 272–276.

Spampinato, MV. et al., Neural correlates of anxiety in healthy volunteers: a voxel-based morphometry study. J Neuropsychiatry Clin Neurosci. 2009 Spring; 21(2):199-205.

Suarez, EC. et al., Enhanced Expression of Cytokines and Chemokines by Blood Monocytes to in vitro Lipopolysaccharide Stimulation are Associated with Hostility and Severity of Depressive Symptoms in Healthy Women. Psychoneuroendocrinology. October, 2004.

Surkina, I. D. et al., 2001. Relationship between IFNγ production by blood lymphocytes and constitutional personality features of patients with idiopathic mitral valve prolapse. *Bull. Exp. Biol. Med.* 131:389– 391.

Walker, E., et al., Psychosocial factors in fibromyalgia compared with rheumatoid arthritis: II. Sexual, physical, and emotional abuse and neglect. Psychosomatic Medicine. 1997;59(6):572–577.

Xu, J. et al., (2011). White matter integrity and five factor personality measures in healthy adults. *NeuroImage, 59*(1), 800–807.

More books by Anne Angelone

Gifted Intelligence

The Autoimmune Diet

If The Buddha Had an Autoimmune Disease

The Autoimmune Paleo Breakthrough

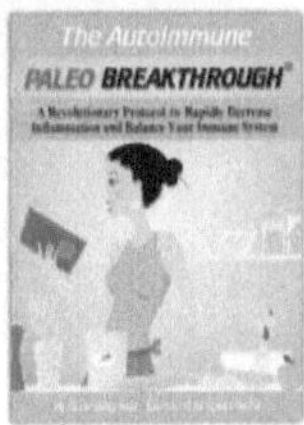

The Paleo Autoimmune Protocol

The Histamine Free Paleo Breakthrough

The FODMAP Free Paleo Breakthrough

Safe Supplements For Autoimmune Disease

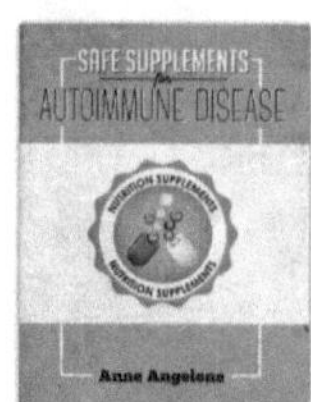

The 10 Day Detox With Real Food

Gut Clear

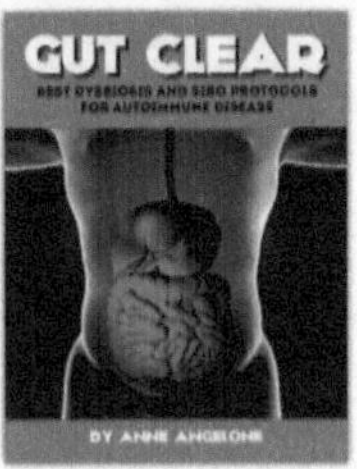

Type G Personality

Beyond Cannabis